> When the suffering of another
> creature causes you to feel
> pain, do not submit to the initial
> desire to flee from the suffering
> one, but on the contrary, come
> closer, as close as you can to
> her who suffers, and try to help
> her.
>
> Leo Tolstoy

Meeting with the twin flame is one the most intense relationships an individual can experience. Contrary to popular belief, the relationship does not necessarily involve romance. Twin flames appear, so as to facilitate personal development, but the relationship does not have to move beyond the platonic stage. The reason for meeting the twin flame serves a specific purpose. An irresistible magnetism develops in both, a feeling that could be misinterpreted according to the circumstances and needs of a particular person. However, the attraction might not but it does not have to create a physical, passionate affair.

The relationship characterises by a powerful fascination for the other person; but also by a misleading sense of rejection. However appealing it might be, both people could be at a stage in their personal development in which they are not ready to bare the intensity or the alchemy experienced with another. It could coincide with the time in which one of them, or both could be in a committed

1

relationship. Rejection intensifies by a sense of knowing and not knowing at once. Such ambivalence is perceived unconsciously. This moment could be described as the memory of an experience that has not yet occurred, but giving the impression that it has already happened. It is possible that one or even both people have not developed a high enough level of consciousness that allows the relationship. Meeting and getting together could take weeks, months, years or it might never happen. It could also be a brief encounter to simply deliver a message, or a life lesson that is required for personal growth. People often seek love as a break from their own life. A life that might be filled with an array of toxic elements, such as substances, unhealthy habits or a number of lovers from which one has not separated energetically. These energies are neither inviting, nor magnetic to attract the kind love someone desires. It is the moment of truth, in which someone has to face the consequences of the choice the made up to that point. Although it does not stop people from engaging in a relationship, it might prevent a twin flame from it. The reason will become clear in this text, as the twin flame journey is explained. By changing perspectives or how someone interacts and responds to the constant stimuli of the twin flame, it is possible to remove personal blockages, allowing to materialise a relationship that up to that moment may only seem evasive.

For the purpose of this book the narrative focuses on the romantic experience, with the intention to bring clarity on the figure of the twin flame. It does apply to any gender, same gender and/or any other type of defined or undefined relationship. Souls do not differentiate gender. Twin flames are agents of change having a great impact in the life of their partner. As a catalyst for personal transformation, the reason twin flames come together is to break a dynamic of unhealthy habits. It allows self-reflection in order to introduce a personal truth that has so far been concealed in the form of habits, beliefs, behaviour and actions as a result of the composite of who one has become. The twin flame arrives with a colourful, vibrant invitation to a new life.

The revelation of truth is introduced through mutual reflection. Both twin flames act as mirrors. Each one showing the other, as well as to themselves, what they have to see, feel and experience in order to grow. Truth reveals itself through action, behaviour and the crumbling of personal beliefs. In the presence of the twin flame false aspects begin to fade. The levels of pain and suffering experienced during the process are proportional to the degree of resistance offered by each individual. However, neither pain, nor suffering are necessary. The fast pace in someone's personal transformation might be overwhelming, as several realisations could take place on a daily basis. One does not have to suffer when aware of the process or what steps to take. Everyone is strong enough to take on the challenge. Not everyone might know this fact about themselves. The role of the twin flame is not to denounce or vocalise your flaws, but to impersonate them, as if they were a mimicking reflection. A reflection of love, and an invitation to come closer by opening to a new perspective. Love is ever growing. It does not end to flow the moment two people choose to start a relationship. The relationship is the beginning. It requires constant energy. What energy one brings into it is a matter of choices.

Such intensity might not be an experience anyone is willing or ready to face; and one or maybe both decide to remove themselves from a love story they have been craving for their entire lives. Contradictory feelings alone can give the impression of insanity. It is not the case. This storm of overwhelming feelings, emotions and beliefs which are constantly challenged has a simple explanation. Once awareness is created, it becomes much easier to enjoy an engaging and exciting relationship.

Personal transformation and self-knowledge entails the disintegration of the self. Let's pause here. The terms of personal transformation and self-knowledge is the natural course of life. People either grow organically through accepting the essence of the experience or wither resisting what life brings. One does not need to follow a spiritual practice, a personal or transformational program in order to develop or to become a better person. Some people chose specific practices for such purpose, while others follow their intuition in the most practical and pragmatic fashion. Both approaches, and any other in between are equally valid. The key is adaptability.

The process of transformation, as well as the wonderful results that someone may experience during a relationship with a twin flame is one to be celebrated, not feared. The reality of the new you will be better, and would feel better than what it may be left behind. A period for self-reflection in order to adapt to abrupt changes may be necessary. With any personal change, not only the present ones, but also the future; enabling to foresee someone's expansion, as well as the possibilities ahead. Healthy modifications in character, personality and the subsequent responses are the keys to new doors. Whatever the outcome, the twin flame materialises to enrich life. Twin flames do not only appear to people following spiritual practices. Love does not make distinctions on people's choices in life. Love is everyone, for everyone and it touches everyone when allowed.

The presence of, and the close interaction with the twin flame accelerates the transformational process. It is a period in which one embodies new personal, energetic truths such as the embodiment of courage. Courage to love. Love as it expands open new doors to truth. As one surrenders to a new truth or self-revelation, courage serves as a vessel to keep afloat in a turmoil of feelings and emotions. The boat does not sink. It might get flooded by waves of truth. It might go through emotional storms, and one might have to change direction, but it is a safe space to navigate. It is also a period to face demons and fears, to transcend what is no longer needed. It is a time to learn to love others, but also self-love and self-acceptance. Some things may not be possible to change, as not everything has to be changed. Whether an aspect of the self can be changed or not is in most cases a personal choice. The twin flame experience is at once, a journey within, a love story, and the possibility of one of the most wonderful human adventures. By entering into the unknown, one might experience the intensity of feelings and emotions that one finds difficult to handle at the beginning of the process. Not all feelings will be negative. Love is also intense, deep; expansive.

It is also a period for love and joy. Love expands acting as a vehicle that creates a complicit synergy between both lovers. What has been experienced in previous relationships is no longer valid. It is time to move on, to learn new ways to be, and/or to interact with others, as well as with ourselves.

The twin flame relationship requires a new form of personal and mutual cognitive and emotional intelligence. Any romantic relationship benefits from such approach. Letting go of the old in order to meet the new in the dynamics of the relationship might bring the sensation that one constantly has to catch up with events, thoughts and ideas. However negative it might sound, the sense of disengagement from the old self indicates a fast track in the right direction. Feelings and emotions might tell otherwise, but these are the right steps towards surrendering the ego, so as to embody an upgraded version of the self. Personal development has to be understood as wanting more and better. Often surrendering to the truth and accepting flawed traits is used as a weapon for self-criticism. There is no point in keeping such attitude. Everyone does their best with what they have. Mistakes are made. One either learns from them or use each one to keep themselves small. Mistakes are part of being human. If we knew better, we would do and act better. What is true today, does not have to be true tomorrow.

Each situation holds a negative and a positive. The possibility to choose one or the other lies on personal perspectives and choices. It is important to remember to have as much fun as possible. Love and life are supposed to be naturally fun. Hear the echoes of the laughter of children. You were once one of those children and still are. Perhaps all it takes is to remember to laugh again, play with the experience. Playfulness is curiosity as its best. New feelings and emotions do not have to be a reason for suffering. The support of your partner is a constant, although true support can only be found in the strength and knowing within, which is one of the hidden treasures the twin flame relationship brings. One cannot constantly rely on someone else's shoulder.

When the twin flame turns up there is an immediate, obvious attraction. Words are not necessary at this stage. It is possible that they observe each other from a close distance, yet, experiencing no separation. If an interaction took place, it could be brief, as if saving the quality time for the moment in which the scenario is more appropriate. Intimacy recognises the perfect timing. A moment worth waiting for. At this point, the sensation of familiarity grows. However, this feeling is not exclusive to twin flames. While curiosity grows on both parts, knowing that the meeting is inevitable, there is a charming dance of souls waiting to interact for the first time. There is no rush. The soul knows of a patience that the human being is not accustomed to yet. Patience settles in, gently taking over. It is at once, an enticing and bothersome feeling, as both souls teach each other patience. Patience prevents emotional reactions. Emotional reactions are impatient, the actions of the inner child, voiced in caricaturesque tantrums. A sense of relief flows in the knowing of mutual recognition. With all probability, the first interaction will be an exchange of meaningful glances at a close distance. However, twin flames are magnetic and spontaneous. Getting together from that moment on is feasible.

What happens next is the beginning of magic and alchemy in the physical realm between two souls at the preamble of a relationship that has neither end, nor beginning. Egos will try to sabotage and destroy the relationship whenever possible. While ego is proud and happy to share its new, beautiful love with the world, there is also an underlined preoccupation for its future existence. The twin flame and the ego simply do not match. One is liberating, the latter is a jailor. Yet, ego will be at its strongest, presenting a fierce battle to preserve identity. Throughout the book, the reader will find recommendations to deface and transform identity in safe ways.

The prevalence of ego in the relationship is punctual, but when appearing, it does so with a vengeance, as all fears and demons gather together in a wild dance in days and nights that one might never forget. As emotions run high, ego finds and deliberately creates opportunities to show its best. Ego's best is a person's worst, and while neither lover wants to hurt the other, hurt might be inevitable after all. Expect heated arguments, fights. It is essential to pay attention, to respond with a new attitude. Pause and awareness prevents most disagreements. Emotional reactions often cause irreparable damage with the consequent loss of trust. Silence is a powerful tool to wrap one's own pride with. Silence brings unprecedented rewards. Not taking a step before a challenge is often a step forward, not backwards. It makes it possible to turn a negative into a positive.

At the beginning, a deep sense of peace flows through body and mind. The soul makes its presence felt. An inexplicable sense of nostalgia for something they never had, and at once, for something lost turns into stillness. It is a connection with the inner self. The real work towards the final connection with the higher self begins here, in stillness. How the relationship develops from this moment on determines present experiences, as well as those in the near future. How we act now sets a precedent for future actions. It could be a lifetime of togetherness or one in which the only thing that remains is the essence, memory, feeling and energy of each other.

While curiosity brings twin flames together, there is also an innate resistance to getting closer. Whether they are single or not, there is an irresistible desire to being near the other. The intention might not be clear at the beginning. Meeting the twin flame is a time of confusion and uncertainty in which the contradictory nature of false self becomes evident. One may feel, and is emotionally naked before a human mirror. Both people want to show their best, while in an inexplicable exhibition of irrationality and contradiction they might do the opposite.

However powerful the mutual attraction might be, the window of opportunity that leads into a relationship is small in comparison, and it might not present itself often. The reticence to establish a closer union is more accentuated than that from any other relationship. Trust might be an obstacle in the earlier stages while getting to know each other, sharing intentions, dreams, or conversations about the possibility of togetherness. It is an emotional negotiation reflected in the obvious reticence to compromise. Once someone enters within the energetic field of the twin flame, defence mechanisms raise all alarms. This can be understood from the knowing that the twin flame is an identical mirror that reflects all the good qualities one may have, but also every flaw, which often translates into similar unhealthy habits and views on life. Each of these chosen traits are an escape from the self. It could lead to two people being in love to separate in order to preserve what appears to be their challenged sanity or to simply recover their vital energy. Ego is a scheming entity which will do anything necessary to preserve its known identity. It would destroy any loving relationship without hesitation to merely prove its righteousness. Ego is always wronged by others.

At this stage it is important to be aware of the fact that any weakness that the body may experience enables the mind create responses that increase ego's resistance. Thoughts of self-preservation appear, hence, ending the relationship might seem the only viable solution. As feelings and emotions are overwhelming, resistance to change invites periods of inaction. Fear of losing a lover person is also manifested in different forms. As tiredness submits the body to a torturous process of paralysis and indecision, the mind becomes ego's most powerful tool generating negative thoughts. The human mind feels comfortable producing this type of thoughts in a futile attempt to manipulate reality. Love cannot be manipulated. Manipulation of the other is a sign of weakness; traits that the twin flame will not tolerate. The freedom that is desired for the self, when projected to any situation could return with unexpected and wonderful surprises. Negative thoughts require as much energy as positive thoughts, but as the relationship reaches a new phase, indulging in negativity is rationalised by a mind that is as exhausted, as the body is. This feeling might be confused with depression and manifested as such. It is not. It is a shadow part in the growth process however uncomfortable it may feel. Becoming aware of our breathing, and making conscious allows relaxation, awareness and expansion. This is an exercise that can be carried out anywhere, any time. Breathing is a natural tool for expansion.

Anyone going through a period of passivity can justify inaction by means of tiredness or exhaustion. As the mind entertains doubts and worries, fear activates a slow process of paralysis that imprisons the natural, expansive expression of the body. This is an energetic prison. Vital energy is used to feed negative thoughts creating more worries, more doubts. Such feelings are usual during a period of growth in personal development. Paradoxically, the antidote to it is action, physical activity, love and self-love. Conscious breathing encompasses all three.

The twin flame is not only an identical mirror. Feelings and emotions amplify, reason for which when or if the relationship enters this stage, the general feeling of discomfort may be overwhelming, even unbearable. Feelings intensify. When feelings and emotions reflect love, understanding and harmony between two people, the world witnesses a period of magic and alchemy. It causes both, admiration and envy. With their presence, twin flames transform energy revitalising spaces. Such phenomena is not only visible to them, but to everyone else. Whereas, during negative periods, darkness takes over, and is not only exchanged between each other, but amplified, changing the dynamic of the relationship. It is a confusing time crammed with contradictory feelings, promoting internal debates in which questions, and the need of survival may resurface. Intensity alone could be the end of the relationship. Both twin flames realise that love is not meant to hurt; that it might not be love after all. It is a crucial moment. One that has no logical answers. No previous experience in relationships prepares anyone for this.

During this period, the twin flame is only one short step away from the complete disintegration of the self. At this point what is required is to trust the other as one never trusted before, to lead with the heart. The heart is where the leader lies. The twin flame experiences a sense of vertigo standing at the edge of an inner abyss that leads to reconnecting with the soul and universal love. In love and in darkness, twin flames continue shining together. Running away from any relationship it is running away from yourself. Hurt is unavoidable in the human experience. Trying to prevent it is a natural reaction to fear. Fear is the route of pain and suffering. To avoid it only brings more of the same. It is also a path that leads to more pain, suffering and self-destruction.

Pain, suffering and disappointment are part of any relationship. Stay with the pain, so as to avoid suffering or the negative thoughts that follow. These episodes are presented to allow the individual to transcend the self in order to evolve. Let go of the need of control. One has to get used to the new level of intensity, ride it as a wild horse that does not need to be tamed, but ridden wild. When allowed, intensity takes us towards a fresh horizon and the multiple possibilities which are found in the unknown. The twin flame appears in someone's life to help us evolve. All periods of transformation, even in love are preceded by chaos. This is a significant element and one of utmost importance, as chaos can be confused with different states of being or feelings. Love continues being the prevalent feeling. If situations become too unpleasant, one must remember that it is a mutual feeling, that your partner also requires support and understanding. Try to see it from their point of view. What one feels, the other does too. It is essential to continue loving, as love is what eventually allows the relationship to settle and blossom. There is not a set time for love to take over. One does not have to wait weeks or months. The time is now. Treat the situation with love to bring results immediately. Be patient and know that it might be a slow process. If the relationship has begun, one can focus on the fact that you both stand emotionally naked and humanely flawed in front of each other. But even flawed, and imperfect in your eyes, he or she are in love. That is perfection; a privilege. In love, there is nothing to fear.

Debunking the Myth

In recent years there has been an abundant influx of literature on this subject, in which such figure has substituted the soul mate. While twenty or thirty years ago people sought to find their soulmate, nowadays most people seek a twin flame, as if it was a birth right. There is no reason not to meet, but it is important to realise that it is an encounter that only takes place when one is prepared to receive and grow. There is no guarantee that it will happen in this lifetime. Anyone can see a reflection of themselves in others. When getting closer to someone else and getting to know them, it is almost impossible not to love others. This can lead to the illusion that the person one has focused their attention on is their twin flame. It might be the case, but it might not. The belief that this might be their twin flame stands against the essence of love. There is not mine, yours or theirs. Language often plays tricks to the speaker. Thus the beauty in silence and self-reflection.

The saying, "silence is full of answers" is understood with perspective and awareness of its meaning. When the mind is calm and silent, one is not listening to constant and pointless inner conversations. As these conversations cause emotional reactions that could lead to anxiety, fear or depression, someone responds with silence to stimuli they remain unreactive. It is the mind that triggers the reaction. Emotional reactions do tend to be followed by impulsive actions that do not always bring the best outcome. Becoming accustomed to a non-reactive new behaviour, is a sign of renewal, as well as an opportunity to a new life. Thoughts change and so does perception, which allows to find alternative ways to deal with reality. It might not be easy to calm the mind, but it is possible with trained thought and meditation.

As humanity moves towards higher consciousness, people are becoming more aware of what is important and what is not. Every day more people are creating healthier spaces, physical, practical, spiritual and energetic in order to allow the integration of more conscious, lasting and fulfilling relationships and life in general. Following heart and intuition is an essential channel to connect with the twin flame. It is an energetic call. This last statement is as obvious as overlooked. Only the heart can open up the possibility of love. The route towards higher consciousness is an individual path filled with highs and lows, as well as periods of wholeness and happiness. In time the feeling and clarity become steady.

In order to do so, one must shed old beliefs that no longer serve, neither the individual, not the whole of humanity. While life could be, and it is indeed fairy tale like during a period of higher consciousness, society must begin to separate from the romantic idea of prince charming coming to the rescue, or of a Damsel in distress waiting to be rescued. The notion that there is a perfect match for everyone or that such person is waiting and in fact will find their way to us is founded on old myths and the vision of romantic love projected by the Disney factory. All relationships are compatible when both people make an effort, a desire to grow together. One does not have to wait for the twin flame or a soul mate to come and brighten up life. Each individual is one part of a collective soul. No one is better or worse than the other. A fulfilling relationship is possible with anyone when love is present.

Understanding the concept of unity is essential in order to raise both, individual and collective consciousness, as it is a necessary step to enable the twin flame to appear. The importance of spiritual "ascension" and manifesting the twin flame will be covered briefly in a different chapter. At this stage the attention is focused on debunking the myth that twin flames appear regardless of actions, life style and state of consciousness.

The collective belief that the twin flame is a birth right is as damaging to a person, as the false expectations created by any other wrong idea. Living in hope for the twin flame to materialise because this is the idea that currently occupies the collective mind can be harmful to anyone seeing that years pass by and the dream of the promised soul mate or twin flame never arrives. It could lead to depression, hopelessness, addictions, low self-esteem or a general sensation of worthlessness. This is a matter of utmost importance, as the feeling of not being loved is one of the main reasons for the low state of consciousness that clouds humanity's reason. It does have negative effects on physical and mental health also.

Everyone is lovable. Everyone is deserving of love. There are no exceptions. If humanity could pause for a while, stand in silence and look into the eyes of another without fearing to show who they truly are or what others may think, everyone would recognise their soul in the eyes of others. The connection with someone else at a soul level is one of the most beautiful experiences a human being can have. Deep human connections are rare, as humanity has learned to distrust each other, and yet, they happen every day to those who dare to open their hearts. The opportunity to create this kind of connection with anyone is ever present. As we distrust others, we distrust ourselves. The energy that goes out, also goes in. Many people are looking for love conditioned by the idea or belief that others will make us complete. This phenomena is based on false beliefs. If there was any truth to such belief, everyone would be in a healthy and fulfilling relationship by now. Distrust of others currently extends throughout the world like a plague leaving a desolate trail of loneliness. If steps are not taken to create a more conscious and organic society, loneliness will be the most extended, chronic disease in the near future.

People do not show who they are because of past hurts. Even if these memories vanished from the conscious mind, the body and the subconscious mind do remember. As a norm, hurt comes from loved ones at a stage in their lives in which one does not have the capacity to rationalise the actions of others. No matter how loving parents may be, their line of thinking and behaviour are most likely clouded by the collective unconscious. The process is simple: stay safe, go to school, grow up safe and healthy, find a job, find a girl or a boy and settle down. It is the stage in which parents know best, if not everything. The question that raises even if not articulated is this: if those who were supposed to love and protect me can hurt me so, what will strangers do to me? The result is distrust. Trusting others take courage. If by giving trust, what is received in exchange is betrayal or hurt one can only remove themselves from the situation knowing that they were true to their heart and the courage that takes to expose themselves to others. It is not a reflection on you, but on others. Not everyone feels comfortable around love or the freedom that offers. The familiarity with the energetic prison in which many people incarcerate their authenticity often disallows safe and healthy spaces for love to grow. Preserving this space in which identity feels safe is the cradle of selfishness. Selfless love and vulnerability represent too much of a threat.

The social construct induces a subconscious set of beliefs that parents use to educate their children to the best of their abilities, but also to project their fears and insecurities by making plans and setting goals with the intention to enable them to adapt and function in a dysfunctional world. Lack of freedom begins the moment parents project an imaginary future on their children, creating expectations before the child has developed an idea of who they want to be. Hurt appears due to the clash of two worlds. The adult and unconscious world and the enlightening reality of children whom are born with a deep, strong connection to the soul and love. If you do not belief in souls, focus on love. They are one and the same, a part of collective consciousness, a state of pure energy. These two ways of understanding life are incompatible, speaking different languages, which inevitably leads to the soul to withdraw to a place of safety. Authenticity is hidden as one becomes more self-conscious. This is the moment in which the inner child appears to engage in a fierce battle with the world, but also against the real self. The inner child never grows. They never forget.

It is a defence mechanism intended to protect the most valued and beautiful expression of the soul, which in time turns into automatisms hard to perceive. The behaviour is in most cases unconscious becoming an intrinsic part of humanity's social dysfunction. It is detrimental to the evolution of humanity, as well as to that of the development of individuals, thwarting the possibility of integration and unity: one voice, one heart, one soul. It is who and what we are, part of the whole. One might face all sorts of dangers, or being subjected to the wrongdoings of others in their human experience, naturally leading people to adopt defensive attitudes. The truth is that the soul is always protected. One should never refrain from showing authenticity.

Another fact to be aware of, is that authenticity is impossible to hide. It does show when someone is distracted. It is the child within, free and in love. It shows with a smile, with a gesture or with a simple expression in moments of self-reflection. Moments of solace help to create this connection. What it might appear to be invisible to the self, it is in all probability visible to others.

Authenticity, however, suffers imprisonment while an individual is seeking constant validation from others. The more one depends on the validation of people, the less likely it is to express it, making them vulnerable to criticism, which in turn weakens confidence and self-esteem. Living under the oppressive belief which constantly hammers the human psyche with the idea that one is incomplete or not good enough triggers such defence mechanisms, conditioning the expansion of the soul or the development of a person. In order to change this type of behaviour one must allow vulnerability, so as to recognise and feel their own truth. One's personal expansion is the integration of their energy with others and the environment. To allow vulnerability is not an invitation to take any form of abuse. One must know when to set boundaries and put a stop to certain types of behaviours in others. Expansion is an extroverted action that can only occur through others, while at the same time it is necessary to find the ideal balance that allows moments of self-reflection and creativity that one produces while alone.

Protecting the soul might seem a valid response to survive in a world that looks and feels unkind, but at the same time creates an energetic field, which stops the magnificent expression of the soul to express its infinite creativity, which is indispensable for its expansion, so as to reach a permanent state of bliss and to live a fulfilling life. In bliss, one is at peace with the world, and most importantly, with the self. At reaching such inner state, one sees life and others as whole. Although the intention is to feel protected, we cannot protect the soul, a source of energy that is stronger and more powerful than the human being. It is through the integration of our inner resources that the soul is protected. It is another paradox. The systematic attempt to protect it, halts the expansion of the soul. A strong sense of responsibility towards others develops a new path of personal truth and integrity. In this journey, one enjoys the qualities of universal love and universal truth. What one might want to consider in terms of thoughts is that if it has not worked so far, it might be time to question our own rationale, and maybe find alternatives ways to live.

It is important to understand that all actions generate energies that affect body, mind and soul. These energies have also an immediate effect on someone's ability to function and communicate, not only with the world, but with the self. The repetitive inner conversation of incompleteness, inevitably identifies external validation as the only support, which in this case is to seek love through others, leading to co-dependant relationships, but also to prove the world wrong when the opportunity to express authenticity has vanished. The love you seek is already within. The road to love must go through self-love, and it is only possible through a journey within. In a relationship, we learn about ourselves through interactions with others.

The twin flame figure accelerates this process. It is a magic moment. When it occurs it is easy for both people to recognise it. Their complicity allows the most authentic part of each to show without fear or restrictions. Life becomes less serious. The love affair is also a playground of dreams in which everything is possible. Under the influence of their presence and mirroring, the relationship turns into the perfect scenario to expose and discredit false beliefs. It could take months, even years before the relationship reaches a peaceful period. But it could also happen within seconds if both surrender to reality seeing it as the space for possibilities yet unknown, and understanding the need for growth they commit to work on consolidating the relationship.

The internet and the use of social media caused the expansion of the idea of the twin flame, to the extent that most people are only willing to attract and settle for this image of perfection. Everyone else becomes unimportant. Other people become unworthy of love in their eyes, and as one projects this belief on others, so do they. Seeing others as lovable does not equal beginning a relationship. This attitude and belief is both a paradox and a trap. A loveless projection on others creates feelings of unworthiness within leading to a loveless existence. It is judgment. The energy emanating from an individual is the same they function with. It is not an energy that attracts love. It is possible to be in a relationship and still hold a feeling of emptiness or loneliness. At the same time, seeing others as worthy of love may give the impression that one falls in love with as many people as they deem lovable. One knows when the feeling is real, as they know when someone is compatible or if the relationship has a lengthy life span. It only means that one is open to love; and love, which is patient knows to wait for the right person at the right moment.

As mentioned earlier, the meeting of twin flames occurs at a time in which both are ready to shed old beliefs and embrace the new. It could be argued that one is always ready, as this statement is true. The only requirement is the courage to take the plunge. Reducing intention to words, ideas and wishes may not suffice to attract the twin flame. One must walk the talk, take action. The meeting could happen in multiple ways. The twin flame could be waiting at the other side of the country or even in a different one. Sedentary life or a life of conformity does not lead to loving reunions. Conformity is an energetic agreement with what we already have. Expecting more becomes an illusion, as it does not open doors for our desires to arrive or to come true. It is unlikely that the twin flame knocks at someone's door to make this magical meeting possible. One must be a true seeker, follow intuition. It is the path to your true essence.

Considering the level of consciousness and apathy the world is in, the majority of people will not meet the twin flame in this lifetime. Let's not see consciousness as an abstract bestowed only to the chosen ones, but as a new state of being that occurs as one returns to their essence. You have already been there, felt it and lived it, even though you might not remember it. However, no one should be discouraged, or to believe that the encounter will never take place. There are not absolute statements. Possibilities are presented every day for the energetic shift to occur. Everything can change in a second. Anything is possible. This book is written to provide information on the subject, as well as holding the intention to be a guide that helps one seeker to meet another. Everyone is seeking in different ways, although at times life circumstances take a toll and one may temporarily stop and retrieve from the world. In addition, someone could be experiencing a low level of consciousness and constricted by false beliefs when the twin flame shows up. Their role is to help to demystify social conditioning, so as to gain freedom and follow their true expression. In love, the path becomes an easier and more fulfilling experience. The appearance of the twin flame sparks the heart. From that moment on, anyone can clearly see the intention and the path to become a better person.

One of the problems the world faces with the overload of information available, although not all, is that in the age of information, humanity still chooses to be misinformed. Information is not sought to seek truth, but to confirm what one already knows. The idea that we can find the twin flame online could be nothing but projection fuelled by an acute sensation of loneliness or feeling lack of love. Anyone can introduce and present an incredible profile online that matches all the characteristics of the twin flame. Such occurrence has a very easy explanation. Most people are looking for love. To express intention matches the intentions of others as, no one is that different from the rest. We simply have different ways to perceive and express it. On paper, intentions are always be good. Deep within we are all the same. That some people forgot what they wrote on that piece of paper is another story.

The mystification of the twin flame also leads to create the wrong idea on such figure. Popular belief has substituted soul mates for twin flames, creating a collective thought that their role is to arrive, fall in love, settle and live happily ever after. This could be possible in a world that believed in love and magic. This world does not, or it does not yet. The role assigned to the twin flame varies ostensibly from it, and there will be a detailed description in one of the following chapters, as well as to why the twin flame might not be willing to settle in a relationship. Twin flames might wish to stay and indeed do so.

Such conception has led many people to think that they met their twin flame, when in fact they have not. Love is love and should not be reduced to one idea, one term or one principle. We are here to love; to remember love. To remember love is the ability to let it grow within in terms of energy and to allow the feeling to flow outwards. Not being able to love those people who are here now, does not create a solid base to love anyone else in the future, especially someone, like the twin flame on whom so much expectations have been placed. These expectations create the idea, as well as an incredible pressure, as someone who has just appeared in someone's life is intended to do all the work for ourselves. It makes meeting the ultimate goal. The end, not the beginning. Humanity has created already too many labels to identify everything, hardly dipping into the true nature of anything, which in turn stops a clearer understanding. Love does not need to be neither labelled, not described. Love is a state of being. A verb we live. For this reason, the idea can become an obsession, which in all certainty will take over the mind, making an individual to seek love through mental projection only. It could also be counter-productive if one of the lovers is obsessed with the notion of the twin flame, which in time could make them to disregard their current relationship for no good reason. Using the ideal of love as an excuse not to love someone else is not love, but a convenient trick to please ego.

Living with a feeling of inadequacy, loneliness or lack of love creates, both, personal and collective neurosis, creating a demand, but also an offer. There is an incredible power in vulnerability, but there is also the unscrupulous character willing to exploit such vulnerabilities for commercial purposes and in exchange of large sums of money that assure to have the secret to every human frailty. A person going through certain states of vulnerability, such as loneliness or lack of love is prone not only to buy into it, but to believe anything they are told. This is how religions built their following. When an 'expert' offers assurance that the person they have been inquired about is in fact their twin flame, they can also convince themselves that it is indeed true, regardless of what the truth might be, so as to wake up years later to realise that it was nothing but a nudge, an induced illusion. When you meet a twin flame, you will know. There is no need to ask anyone else.

Throughout life people are attracted to many people. It is not surprising. People are beautiful, and when we take the time to look deeper, even more so. To fall in love is natural in the human experience. We can learn so much from others, whether they are a soul mate, a twin flame or any other concept one holds in mind or true to their heart. As with vulnerability, silence also holds an incredible power. Silence of the mind, without words, thoughts or ideas. The noise of the world is overwhelming, clouding consciousness. Unfortunately, everyone contributes to it. It is possible to live in a world without words, communicating through feeling, in silence. When the mind is calm enough, everyone can communicate telepathically with anyone else regardless of their location. In the same way, one can also communicate and listen to the wisdom of universal knowledge.

One of the next chapters details the description of the twin flame, what their role is and why they appear. Debunking the popular myth of the twin flame is written with the intention to bring clarity to the subject, as well as to encourage the individual to seek through their own intuition and natural resources, which are plentiful once we tap into them. To believe in love and magic is one thing, but to infantilise the romantic figure of the twin flame by allowing the inertia of previous eras to promote false beliefs around love or who one must love is an unhealthy habit. In other words. Stop waiting and go and get it. People only find their true power when it is used. Seeking guidance or reading references helps in building ideas or learning concepts, but everything is subjected to interpretation and experience. One might recognise truth in this book, but it does not have to become an absolute. Everything in life is in constant movement. A reference is not the end, but the beginning of an experience that has to be explored with experience.

The evolution of humankind requires developing beyond old and false beliefs, which have not contributed anything to the betterment of the world. Romanticising the figure of the twin flame could compare to the story of Moses and the 'Promised Land', one he saw, but in which he could never enter. Being infatuated by the idea can lead to a lifelong disappointment and heartbreak, making an individual to miss opportunities of true love. Somehow the world lives under a spell of a false sense of entitlement. Meeting with the twin flame is not guaranteed. That certainty does not exist, as it is not true that anyone is meant to live a loveless life. But what does not exist can be created. We create such opportunities seeking through experience. Experience brings confirmation of who we are. Perhaps this is not the time to meet the twin flame. There are no guarantees that they will remain either. There is no certainty. Forget safety and certainty and you will be several steps closer to find love. The human experience is characterised by change. Change is that wild horse that cannot be tamed, but ridden wild, as the soul would do. In love.

Meet people organically

In recent years, modern technology and the Internet had a major influence in people's feelings, beliefs about themselves and others, as well as how we communicate with others. The new generations will not understand communication or life without it. Older generations might use these channels differently, but it is still considered a useful instrument that enables immediate communication with others, as well as to satisfy personal needs instantly. When used appropriately, social media is an excellent tool for knowledge and/or to improve communication. How it is used and for what purpose is a personal choice. However, too much emphasis, hope and emotion is invested on social media looking for elements that cannot be transmitted through virtual reality; being this, the feeling and energy experienced when meeting others organically.

One of the detrimental uses of social media is public exposure. In many cases, the online portrait does not match the reality of the subject, allowing for an inaccurate representation of the self, as these are moments captured at a particular time, not an ongoing process. Although it might not apply to everyone, the excessive projection of self-image could be portraying a truth that is tainted by need or loneliness or both. It is easy to maintain an image of strength, harmony and love that could be misrepresenting. Everyone has a bad day, as everyone eventually falls for an emotion and the consequent reaction.

It could be agreed that everyone is a seeker. In fact everyone is to a certain extent. A seeker of love, happiness and wellbeing. Getting distracted from seeking or adopting unhealthy habits is only a step backwards, even if at the moment to get back on track it seems like the beginning again. It is a pause in the process, a time to gain knowledge through self-reflection. These processes might be repeated time and again until a lesson is learned. It is no reason to be discouraged, but one to encourage change. Love is what everyone wants. Until it is found, people get distracted by other activities, material or superficial distractions, or even other people. Not all friendships are based on true friendship, as not all relationships are born out of love. As a whole, humanity lives under the misconception that love is something that is attained through another person. While this notion is somehow true, truth is also that within each individual lies a bottomless source of love which makes the first statement flawed. Anyone can experience love with another person. However, periods in which one is not in a fully committed relationship are often interpreted or misinterpreted, as someone does not deserve love or they cannot have it.

Love is not a feeling exclusive of a relationship. Seeking love through others is never the wrong step to take. Everyone is a teacher. The paradox in the quest for love is that while we seek what we believe we lack, we teach others what we already are and have, as well as teaching ourselves what love is. By teaching others one inevitably learns and remembers who we are. Even when it might seem that one is experiencing lack of it, everyone's internal love compass allows to recognise it. The purpose of the process is a return to love.

How we meet other people is important, not only in regards to twin flame relationships, but to all relationships. While technology allows immediate connection, it also dehumanises the relationships that are established. Technology and social media are neither good, nor bad. What use is made of it determines the nature of the relationships. Only a part of the self can be exposed and transmitted through computerised screens and selective messages. Virtual communication allows an individual to pause, reflect and think in order to either, initiate a conversation or to reply to previous communication at a convenient time, which in turn permits to project the ideal image and the perfect response. Reality changes when two people connecting online meet in person, as the meeting requires an immediacy in their answers and responses. Spontaneity and improvisation are lost in the online universe, which are essential in a face to face meeting. No longer can one use their screen as a refuge. Organic communication requires to be present in the now and here. Words, thoughts, ideas and actions might create a different energy to what is initially intended. While it is appropriate to think through what answers one may give, a face to face meeting may create an energy that has not been foreseen. The more one indulges in online communication, the less spontaneous creativity is. It might not be as easy to present the perfect online portrait of the self without the assistance of a screen. Technology will never be a substitute for the warmth, spontaneity and synergy created when meeting people organically. Nothing can be a substitute for the human touch.

The ability to transmit energy, feelings, emotions or one's essence from any part of the world to another is innate in every human being, as well as being able to communicate telepathically with others. In love, words are not necessary. Dormant senses awaken. Communication reaches an alternative dimension only known to lovers. Everyone is born with this gift. As people age, their energetic field and the ability to project energy is reduced by the association that is being made of love being an external source, consequently disregarding their natural abilities. At entering such stage, communication is limited to the material, the superficial and that what is near: what one can see or touch. Our senses are also reduced to five according to popular belief, when in fact human beings are naturally gifted with over twenty different ones. These are signs that merely indicate that we might not know yet who we are or that we are not fully aware of the amazing abilities innate to every human being. It is a period of disconnection with the world and the true self, in which, consciously or unconsciously individuals embark on a journey to remember, while continuing to inflict upon themselves the teachings and habits learned in childhood. One might adopt eating habits damaging to their bodies, which is one of the most embraced and extended behaviours in modern society, and one which is challenged once again with the ideas and methods of others. Most people seek assistance from professionals and experts, which allows them to understand the problem first, then to find the root of it. Anything but to trust intuition or any of their natural abilities. Again, seeking guidance is a natural and healthy step until it is understood that this is all it is, guidance. One has to do the work themselves.

No matter how disconnected someone might be from their core, the soul never stops whispering wisdom. This is a connection that can be made through intuition, being meditation the practice that allows a faster access to it. In the journey to meet with the twin flame, one must follow intuition even when the reasons are not clear or the path does not make sense to the rational mind. An intuitive insight is not to be confused with the impulse to react to emotions. They are both different in nature. The difference can be easily perceived by the energy that is created and how one feels as a result of their actions, thoughts or words.

The soul is passionate about creativity, expansion, playfulness; movement. When all or some of these four elements are in place, the soul responds manifesting a life plentiful in love and light. In this regard, meeting with the twin flame can be understood as answering the call of the soul. However, one does not have to meet their twin flame in order to learn to love. Love is always here and now. The twin flame might help to identify it or feel it, but this love, this passion are energies that everyone carries within. Instead of following step by step already made courses offered by others, the suggestion is to listen to intuition and follow synchronistic signs during the journey. The twin flame is a person that when ready will be on a journey of self-discovery and adventure following their inner call. The call awakens a passionate urge to seek an inner truth that might be felt, but not seen; a new and powerful sense of direction and knowing. While your twin flame might be making an excellent use of social media, it is also possible that they are actively seeking, not only a relationship, but furthering self-knowledge and personal development. Nothing stops a person from being their own perfect reflection. One does not need to wait for anything or anyone. The answers are already here and now.

Seeking the twin flame or romantic love through social media has a strong component of conformity and stagnation, while a future partner might be leading more organic interactions with others. The mere act of seeking or expecting a twin flame by focusing on a person that may or may not appear narrows down the vision of love and life. It is a vision against the universal. Playing safe does not invite the spontaneity or improvisation that found in the unknown, although it is understandable that personal circumstances may invite to resort to social media for such purpose. Do not conform. The twin flame might not come knocking at your door, nor to your screen. The screen may only be distracting you from your real purpose in life. The adventure begins beyond fear, beyond what we know, and beyond the safety of the mirage of certainty. One must be prepared to be surprised by the limitless opportunities ahead.

Communicating through social media is perhaps too convenient, too safe. It allows to receive a message, giving time to think and reply at a more appropriate moment with an answer that satisfies someone's needs. Meeting people organically requires a higher degree of spontaneity and authenticity. Social media is destroying these skills in people. Making an initial contact through social media is a wonderful opportunity to meet someone that they would have never met otherwise, but that a meeting in person requires different responses for which one may have lost, or even never developed due to communicating through a screen. The screen is based on a familiar environment that frequents personal and familiar answers. It gives a false sense of control. One might feel like a fish out of the water when communicating face to face. There are multiple advantages about online communication, such as creating community, professional collaborations or even finding love. No possibility can be discarded. When people are involved, everything is possible.

Intuition takes us to visit new places or to attend events that are completely out of character, thus breaking familiar patterns and habits. If the twin flame does not turn up at one's door, they might have to go and knock on someone else's door. It is that simple. Someone's door could be the invisible space that someone holds daily sitting at a coffee shop. In this case, and in order to knock what is needed is the courage to enter that energetic field. As one expands through activities, new thoughts and beliefs, they also attract what they seek, including people. Expansion is magnetic, as it involves vulnerability and passion.

At some point life may turn bleak. One might experience periods of hopelessness. However uncomfortable the situation may be, going through it brings relief. These stages are necessary in the process of disintegration of the ego, as well as numbing down the natural resistance of the self in order to change. Going with the flow or responding to adversity with a can-do attitude are essential steps to overcome obstacles.

The general obsession with meeting the twin flame could also lead to project this image on anyone. A curious phenomena, but not rare, is to witness people identifying two or more people as their twin flames over a short period of time. When looking for something specific one might be projecting their intention in order to see what they are looking for. At the same time, there are cases in which someone tries to convince others that they are in fact their twin flames by simply checking an online profile. This occurrence is no different from the process of researching and writing a dissertation which leads to the relevant information in different media. We see what we want to see. We hear what we want to hear. The information gathered might be pertinent to the subject, often useful, but it might not be the essential data that makes an extraordinary dissertation. One might need to continue seeking new information for such purpose. In the quest of love, falling in love is and should be reward enough. Let's not halt the possibilities of love to be presented because the other person might not tick all the boxes. By limiting someone else's abilities with own views, we stop their ability to express openly. Lack of belief in somebody else is an energy that transmits a powerful message draining their vital energy, which in turn may result in them finding a different canvas where to express their passion, their love and their creativity. For this reason people struggle to feel that they are good enough, and it is given and received by most people every day. This feeling might not be articulated, as it is transmitted energetically, but it is essential to understand that this energy sends a clear message: that someone is neither ready to love, nor receive love. Do not allow the search for the ideal person or twin flame to stop you from finding everything else you want. Practice love through self-love. Get excited about the endless possibilities. What we give our attention, energy and intention to is what we get. There are two choices. It is either love or fear.

In addition to the uplifting energy of being in love, under which influence the perspective of any individual changes, opening to an entire new world of possibility, one must consider that in any type of relationship two individuals mirror each other. Any romantic partner may reflect or appear to mirror the same qualities of their lover. However different each individual may be, deep within there is not much difference between people. The essence of the human being is love. When expressed openly, two people involved in a romantic relationship are inevitably bound to see themselves in the other person. The hard part is to allow love to flow.

There seems to be a belief that the twin flame is a person that everyone is meant to meet, a must, so as to live the happily ever after. Such belief corresponds with Disney's love formula that throughout time defined an illusory, standard idea of romantic relationships. The idea that one person alone, twin flame or not, responds to the image of the ideal partner creates an absolute that in time can only generate disappointment. People grow and develop as time goes by. As a consequence, views, ideas and beliefs change, and so do feelings. Such feelings might not necessarily relate to their partners only, but goals and expectations; an inner calling that could cause them to begin a new life away from what is known. This realisation or inner call might involve separation from the twin flame or any other type or romantic relationship. One knows when the relationship begins, never when it ends. Love is an endless adventure that requires the constant use of curiosity in all aspects of life. The question at this point is to reflect on how curious one might be at the present time. This is an easy exercise, as well as powerful and self-revelatory. It is a simple as taking stock of your life, where you are in your emotional state and see whether it is helping to learn something new or not, and if not, when was the last time you were curious about exploring a talent that might have been dormant for years.

To maintain the romantic idea of the twin flame might be detrimental. Once a belief settles firm in the mind, any deviation from the established plan brought upon reality could have devastating effects. Love in its unconditional expression carries no expectations. Beliefs founded on expectations can only lead to deception. To attract love or the twin flame, one must allow. Seeking can turn otherwise into an ironic path, repelling what we seek. Do not allow the idea of the twin flame to become a ghost to be chased for life missing every opportunity to love along the way. Openness brings the unknown, which includes, situations, places, knowledge, experience, people or lovers.

The soul connection with the twin flame is particularly strong, but it does not necessarily the strongest. There is life before, during and after the twin flame. The strength of the connection that is made with others is what and how much everyone allows. Saving yourself for the twin flame, weakens the connection with anyone else. What begins weak cannot last. Such connection is recognisable when meeting, hence the importance of meeting people organically. Through energy one can recognise the reflection of their own true essence in others, what the soul craves to experience. It is two magnets that attract and repel each other. Perfect mirrors in which to see the reflection of everything that someone needs to, or to perceive about themselves, every flaw, every mistake and every erroneous belief that has been learned and adopted as truth from an early age, but also their best expression; the most beautiful and eloquent authenticity. In order to remember who we are, one must identify and forget who they are not. The experience is a fascinating journey; one of mutual, almost irresistible attraction. Twin flames adore each other, as much as they fight each other. At the moment of realising that this represents a fight with the self that is mirrored in the other, one can begin to focus the attention on themselves, setting a new course in life towards personal freedom and love. Twin flames are equals. One is as powerful as the other. Feeling of superiority in any type of relationship or taking anyone for granted is surely a path that leads to a farewell.

Nothing compares to meeting people organically. Anyone that has attended a live event or a party would recognise the excitement in gathering with others. Face to face, people spread their energy as it is, as they feel it at the moment. Presence is the best broadcast of who you are. No time for Photoshop, editing or projecting an image that might be true in their inner core, but one that have not yet been mastered. Meet people organically, be witness to what you see, not to what someone might want you to see. Get out there!

Shadow Work

You see, nothing can
blind me for long, not
even myself. I am too
much aware of my own
heart.

Anaïs Nin

The twin flame relationship provide the appropriate conditions to facilitate the end of ego's ruling, the death of the mundane and superficial, who and what someone may have become, and that which they are not. This is the beginning of end of the shadow self. When interacting with others organically, one obtains information and impressions immediately. It is not that there is something wrong with your character or with you, but that certain traits, beliefs and habits might be halting your from using your true potential. In most cases, a small change creates substantial changes. While one's original reactions might serve the purpose short term, it might not allow change nor growth. One follows their ever changing and growing nature. This is where the adventure is found; in the self. It is an intense process that if dealt with the level of awareness required will see anyone through the complete disintegration of the self and a spiritual rebirth closer a permanent state of being in love. In order to see results, both partners must have a similar level of self-awareness and an understanding of the possibilities in the process. The awareness one has now is enough to take us to the next level of it. It could be an excruciating period; as ego offers an intense resistance to die. Ego is an eager participant in the disappearance of ego or so it may seem. However, ego can only contribute to create a different egotistic image that may create a better public impression, but never an expression of true love.

In addition, all demons and fears will make their presence felt. The course of the relationship demands a tremendous amount of energy. It is a period in which constant choices must be made, due to the fact that such decisions will be against one's own beliefs. There cannot be change if choices continue being as they have always been. Resorting to the same choices equals the same results. The question that everyone must face, not only in a twin flame relationship, but in life in general is, whether to continue living as we have, or if there might be a need to introduce changes. This symbolic death can be a slow process, but one that no one should fear. It is also possible that everything changes in a matter of minutes.

Hidden fears are easy to perceive during this period, as there might have been a lifetime of avoidance. At the same time, it might not be easy to admit to fear. Allowing ego to keep fighting for its survival, results in the end of the relationship. Fear is an illusion. Even if fear is felt, understanding this concept allows to look at it with different eyes. Every fear is a limiting belief, an energy for which we have learned to have an irrational respect that would undoubtedly bring a harmful outcome. In a twin flame relationship avoiding to face or to go through it, might bring the scariest outcome of all. The end of love. Fear appears in different forms, jealousy, envy, anger or hate. This is not who you are, but before we remember who we truly are, we must go through every unwanted feeling and emotion. Avoidance of unpleasant feelings and emotions is the main obstacle in personal growth. The adventure of love and life requires courage, as well as many other elements that everyone already possesses. It takes seconds to go through fear. It is not different from the first time that a child jumps in the pool and learns to swim. If you never learned to swim, compare it to that one time in which you had to ride a bike. It is the belief that one cannot do it, the excruciating hesitation before taking action. It is also important to remember that this is also an adventure filled with love, that one can choose which energy to function with.

It is a matter of exploring and practicing what we have, what and who we are, so as to realise that what you are seeking is already here and has always been here. Going through feelings and emotions, ego suffers, which in turn increases resistance. However, this is taking responsibility, a way to self-parenting. Ego is an irresponsible child refusing to come off of a tantrum. Allowing pain sees the process through. While advancing through the process with sufficient awareness, suffering is optional. Feeling the pain is enough. The reaction to it determines whether one suffers or not. It might not seem as an option, but it is.

The process is easy in theory. When or if feeling jealousy, -to choose an emotion-, the steps go as follows: admitting to it, acceptance and feeling it until it disappears or weakens to the point that it has no control over the individual. The more one feels, the weaker the emotion becomes, the greater the awareness. You become stronger as energy is released. Positive results might not be achieved immediately, as the emotion has probably been growing in strength for years. It takes time and patience to release the energy that has been accumulated throughout life. One might feel depressed. However, it is possible that is not depression, but a momentary energetic reaction to acceptance. As ego weakens, so does body and mind. The body needs to slow down to feel emotions. This is an example of what is known as going into the unknown; to enter an energetic territory created due to a life of avoidance or simply not knowing.

The twin flame relationship is a fertile ground for new insights, appearing often, perhaps not allowing enough time to process. It could create the illusion that one is a visitor in their own being, as if learning to give baby steps towards a different life. This is the ideal time to become the observer. Instead of seeing it as it is happening to you, see that it is happening through you. As a norm, positive change usually requires new forms of expression. The soul is pushing to come through in order to allow a person to live to their own truth, one in which the self reaches the full expression of inner beauty. During this period the only tool that helps to go through it, might be love. Love for ourselves, as well as love for a lover. This involves making a conscious decision to bring truth to the surface, to accept and embrace it. While it might be a painful development, it is also a beautiful transformation that in time brings amazing rewards to any individual willing to separate from the old self.

New worlds emerge as someone separates from the lies that society has led us all to accept as truth. Integrating lies is an unavoidable part of becoming human. Society has not been built with the intention to embrace free spirits or creative individuals, but to guarantee the perpetuation of comfort and safety for the convenience of some. There is neither adventure, nor anything natural in comfort and safety. Risks must be taken. Lies that have been accepted as the standard truth are subtle, often unconscious. It might not be easy to distinguish a lie from the truth, especially if a lie has provided someone with a relative level of successful functioning up to the present moment.

Shadow work is a destructive process. The twin flame feels and perceives lies. Own it, admit it; discard it. When someone has not reached the awareness that permits to identify it as their own, they will project it on their partner. In this scenario there is no place to escape to. There is nothing that can be done to avoid it. Trying to control the process is nothing but a plan devised by ego. Ego cannot fool the twin flame. The ways of the ego may be all one has ever known. The unknown awaits just one second away. If you find yourself in this situation, love, as well as your own life experience will help you through. Eventually you will thank yourself for it. The alternative is to go through this process alone once your lover, tired of the repetitive illusion moves on. It is a choice to make; one that might not be available for too long. If there is one thing the twin flame lacks, that is patience after meeting repeatedly with the same lie. Compassion and empathy allow to remember that they are also going through their own process of self-realisation and that in such emotional state, one might not want to be seen.

There might be a moment in which you no longer recognise yourself. Do not panic. The answers and tools frequently used to deal with different situations will not be there any longer. Take this as a positive, as it renders you reactionless to emotions. You may experience also a lack of vital energy. You are now ready to deal with emotions and release energy from the body. Lack of vital energy is due to the release of energies. The more one resists change when the opportunity appears, the less vital energy one can expect. If the release of energies is too fast, which is a possibility, one might fall ill; perhaps developing a fever, so as the body can rest after the releasing trauma. The emotional state might be uplifted during this episode. It is time to act differently, to develop an alternative approach to engage with the situation. The thinking process changes, one might become less articulate, less talkative. People may become morose, feel weaker. This part of the process should not stop anyone from enjoying quality time. The body needs to pause, rest and regain energy. In this case, sleep is the best remedy. This could be the first opportunity in years to experience personal changes. A time to take baby steps and to get acquainted with different facets of you. New parts that as they show feel familiar, but which might have been missing for years. It is easy to recognise: it feels good.

Shadow work procures numerous reunions with the self. Everyone at one point or another has undergone periods of hardship in which everything seems to go wrong, followed by a new period in which life feels lighter and smoother. It is necessary to take care of yourself, not only during this period. It is a lifetime duty. One can embrace well-being, as one can embrace hopelessness. The choice is yours. Not taking care of ourselves might indicate that one is going through a period of hopelessness at which point one gives up taking no action to improve the situation. Hopelessness, as well as any other state of being lasts as long as anyone wants to. If one approach does not work, it is a matter of trying a different one. Lack of vital energy, depression, negative or self-deprecating thinking might also be indicating that it is a time to do nothing, feel and reflect. The pace and unreasonable demands of society require an extraordinary amount of energy from individuals, which are clearly not dedicated to improve anyone's personal life, nor contribute with any steps for growth. In a social reality in which constant production is an unwritten must, being out the mad wheel gives the false impression of uselessness.

In order to advance in the relationship, avoid arguments, blaming or trying to be right. The new you does not need to be right, just loving. Confrontation only weakens people. What is coming next is better than what it is left behind. Spoken words, as well as the constant need to explain can be exhausting. While physical action, movement and exercise are vital elements in the development of a person, in this case physical energy can be directed to strengthen the body, rather than undertaking practical steps to deal with the demands of the world as a headless chicken because "you have to do". The constant belief that "I have to do" is an exhausting trap, as no matter how much it is produced, it would never be enough. The mind travels faster than the body.

At this stage it is ideal to have an intimate conversation with your partner. Although it might not be easy to articulate everything that one is going through, and there is no need to, it is appropriate to explain these changes to the best of your abilities. It is an ongoing conversation, not one that has to bring immediate answers. There is need for emotional and moral support, love, understanding and compassion. Do not be afraid to ask. Your partner is also your friend. Overall frustration might lead to react negatively to what it may seem the loss of personal identity. Playing this card could have disastrous consequences, as there might not be enough strength left. The destructive process in shadow works affects both partners. Sometimes transformation is swift and painless, others painful and dark. A process could take minutes, hours or days. These periods are temporarily weakening and disabling. But this is another illusion. Without the appropriate direction or awareness of what is happening, or why it is happening, one of the partners might be tempted to end the relationship. In addition to the self-destructive process, one has to consider society's pressure and practical responsibilities.

Modern society exercises an overwhelming amount of pressure on individuals in a variety of ways. None of which are neither healthy, nor subtle. The pressure is to be strong. Only the strongest survive, rumour has it. Collective consciousness is a perfect platform to keep everyone in a low state of consciousness by functioning on false beliefs that continue spreading through clichés. It is not the strongest that survive, but the most adaptable.

The world needs a new education system that reinforces the strength and natural abilities of the individual, as well as creating a solid sense of community from birth. An education based on universal truth that contributes to educate children to grow strong, genderless and free. Love should not be something to remember, but what we are.

Society as a whole acts callously to any sign of weakness, discarding individuals that no longer serve its productive needs without contemplation. The need to be strong at all times in a competitive society weakens body, mind and spirit. Everyone experiences low moods at one time or another. When experiencing low moods, the natural response is to withdraw from the world, and find solace in dark chambers only familiar to them. It is somehow comforting. This could translate into one of the partners removing themselves from the relationship. The body's intuition begins to work calling for self-preservation. Rest and self-reflection are required. Depending on the individual, it is best to do it alone. Lack of awareness of what the process entails might give the impression that the relationship or the other person are to blame. It is easier to blame an external factor than to deal with our own demons. This reaction could be prevented with an intimate and intelligent conversation. Ego will continue to present a fierce opposition, as it is obvious that the relationship is weakening, maybe even fading. Nothing farther from the truth, but not everyone can admit to weakness or vulnerability.

The people who grow healthier and stronger in relationships are those who allow vulnerability in their energetic space. They drop their protective barriers letting feelings and emotions to reach deep. Vulnerability is a wonderful tool in personal development, as it slowly removes what no longer serves an individual by releasing energies, eventually facilitating inner peace. As energies are released and one gains conscious awareness of who they are, new and healthier traits are adopted. One becomes more functional, expressing a wider perspective and greater projection. These individuals are led by an inner intuitive guide that knows that there is nothing worth preserving, even if they are not entirely aware of this fact. They are seeking adventure, guided by a tunnel vision that knows that every present obstacle is an opportunity to get to where they want to be. How they remain calm and vulnerable to such exposure might be intimidating to others due to the difficulty in understanding such composure. In adventures, people, places and situations are left behind. What remains is experience, and with each new experience, new memories, new energy. Most of the negative emotions a person creates are due to lack of experience. Many could be avoided if one followed intuition instead of the first thought or emotional impulse. It is essential to choose wisely what experiences to go through, even though, often, a negative experience might be most revelatory, serving to change beliefs, perspective and behaviour. A person does not necessarily need to have a concrete idea or form of what this new state of being might be. What characterises them is a relentless optimism for a better reality, which would be expressed time and again. Regardless of what circumstances may be, they do feel safe and exercise an incredible amount of patience and understanding towards situations, but also towards others, which ultimately assists them in developing strength in flexibility. Patience, as well as thirst for self-knowledge makes them feel safe somehow. With this understanding, one also knows that there is more to the situation than what meets the eye.

While self-preservation is a natural tendency in humans, it might not be the best place to seek refuge in a relationship. It could, and most likely will become a prison where someone may feel protected, but never safe. This relates only to the emotional spectrum of a relationship, not to be confused with ways of dealing with abuse of any kind. Relationships are a perfect ground to throw caution to the air –within reason- if one wants to grow, both personally and with their partners. It is a time to believe in the sacredness of trust in order to experience new beginnings with a lover. A new relationship is a blank canvass, the perfect opportunity to create the most outstanding piece of art in someone's life. Trying to recycle old paint, pots and brushes might be counter-productive. If the old relationship formula has not worked so far; it is time to let it go.

In this regard, excessive caution causes to build energetic barriers; the walls of one's own prison with the intention to prevent hurt. Preventing feeling and emotions has the opposite effect that one may intend. The pain is already there; now reawakened. The experience that it is created instead is suffering as emotions magnify. Both pain and suffering are associated with or blamed on their partner. The reasoning is that without them, neither would exist. Pain and suffering resurface when least expected with more intensity. It is the moment to decide whether one wants to end it all or to continue hurting. It is the perfect time for healing. Logic tells that if this is love, it is not supposed to hurt. It is a trap, as this is nothing but projecting onto others instead of taking responsibility for their own feelings. Within every problem, there is also a solution. One needs to dig deeper, remain calm and patient focusing on love, which is always present. Love is also a choice. The answer is in what one focuses on. Every second, every minute is an opportunity to change direction towards a better, more peaceful life. Negative feelings and emotions are followed by negative thought, feeding negative energy, which in turn brings more thoughts. It is an endless cycle.

Throughout this text so far there are numerous references to the end of the relationship, as a reminder of a possible outcome. In the same text, there are multiple references to love, as well as the possibilities for personal growth. In fact, positive outcomes are more numerous than the negatives. At this point, you may pause and reflect which one stick in the mind during the reading.

The twin flame appears to tear you apart, not to have a loving relationship for life, even though it is possible. If both go through this process successfully, there is indeed a chance for the relationship to blossom and experience a life of growth and love. Although the purpose of the twin flame relationship is not to linger in time, thus separation is a possibility, but it does not have to end. For the relationship to continue, both have to reach a certain degree of awareness of their emotional body, as well as to control actions, reactions and responses. The problem is that while going through the process, hurt may be too intense, but as one gains knowledge and awareness of the significance of the process, they can look back at those situations with humour and laugh about a more unconscious period in their lives. Regardless of the situation you are facing, the emotions and feelings you might be experiencing, do have as much fun as possible, create touching and wonderful experiences. By reading this book, it is possible to interpret that shadow work in a relationship is an excruciating experience from beginning to end. It is not. These episodes could take place every few days and it might be a repetitive issue, which indicates that as soon as the issue appears, it is necessary to deal with it immediately. In any case, shadow work does not take over the relationship. It is punctual. The example of jealousy given earlier in the text illustrates this. If jealousy were to appear, one admits to it. From that moment on, one is aware of it, and feels it without reaction. Someone is a relationship would be aware if these feelings are based on their partners behaviour or it is simply an irrational emotional reaction. The purpose of this text is to offer guidance on what might happen during the relationship, and as awareness increases, to offer tools that prevent separation or a tense experience. Shadow work is what causes the pain to resurface. Love, what helps to transcend it. Relationships open the space for shadow work to take place, whether someone is aware of the process or not. Awareness of the process could ease the experience.

Regardless of the outcome or the duration of the relationship, the twin flame never forgets. The connection continues in essence. These memories become teachings, reminders of the parts of the self that need to heal. Whether the relationship continues or ends, you keep living, developing and learning. It is not the end. As life improves, people become more magnetic. This effect can be felt in a soul level wherever the twin is. It might be the cause of their return. It is also possible that at some point, you no longer want their return. Trust the process and be patient. People come to us when the moment is right, not when we decide.

Finally, if they have disappeared from your life, do continue loving them regardless of how the relationship developed or ended. Love and let go, then you can have it all. Twin flames are always connected. Know and feel this connection. Love is the most powerful magnet. When you feel and embrace such magnetism, the twin flame might not be what you want.

The importance of shadow work is simple. It brings a deeper understanding on issues that one might have become repetitive patterns in life. Some feelings and emotions are useless, as it is the reactions to them. Shadow work allows to create responses that stop emotional reactions, gaining a sense of inner peace. In time and free of reactions, life becomes a better place. The results can achieve extraordinary transformation.

The One That Got Away

When the twin is a runner, they would do anything to sabotage the relationship. Being in love does not stop them. It does not make sense and it does not have to either. There is nothing anyone can do to stop them if running away if that is what they want. It is all they have known for most of their lives, and even if it is a tactic that does not help to achieve what they want; running feels safe. By this time, they have learned everything about you, but also about themselves. There is nowhere to hide. They know who you are, see your flaws and frailties. You will notice this soon enough. It is time to begin to admit to the truth and heal. Projection interferes. They recognise their own flaws and frailties, even admit to them and they could be rather vocal about it. The problem appears when the relationship is identified as the catalyst for these issues to be ever present. Although they might not blame you directly, finding the strength to face their own demons might not be what they want to use their energy for. To the runner, the experience is debilitating; mentally, emotionally and physically. Alone they would not have to deal with a storm of feelings. Being alone is a safe space for the runner. In the midst of these emotions, they might say things they will regret. Their actions might also leave them numb or over emotional. Bringing shame and guilt on themselves is a self-destructive ritual. How they present the information varies. It either falls on you or blame themselves. Either way, the relationship has to end. What they might say and what their eyes express would most likely be two different stories, but as more importance is given to words than feelings; words is what they will go for. The end of the relationship feels like the end of everything, or so it seems for a while. Love is not always enough, however sad or false such statement sounds. When the end comes, they certainly know which buttons to push. Even if there is no reaction to provocation, they will run away. First the twin flame will try to escape with logic. If such strategy does not work, -and it is a deliberate strategy-, they will follow the irrational way. One way or another they find a way out. Reasons are not important, any excuse suffices.

You might have showered them with love. If so, live in peace knowing that you are not the one to blame for the outcome. The reason to run away is fear of love. What excuse they might find does not matter, as it will be a lie, a truth not spoken with the heart. However, this is what their lover is left to deal with. A lie turned truth and written on the coldest stone. An excess of love is suffocating to them, but not necessarily. Any amount of love provokes the same reaction. Giving all the space in the world would have made no difference. Separation has a devastating effect. This is the real heartbreak. Subconsciously, this is what one was looking for in order to heal completely, to become free. Heartbroken and feeling rejected, the natural reaction is to ask for their return. In theory, this is the opposite of what to do, but the heart does not understand of theories.

The runner is constantly triggered by love, the reason that takes them to run, and as they run, they indulge in the melancholy of longing. The runner needs to pause. What they cannot find in love, they will find nowhere else.

It is time to be alone, to take care of yourself and heal. However, loneliness lands heavy on anyone after separation. Feelings and emotions are overwhelming. It is a very delicate moment in the life of a person. Some people never manage to overcome it, as heartbreak, longing and suffering might become a new false identity. Once the relationship is over, it is essential to let them go. The feeling of belonging together continues being strong, thoughts that no one else will ever understand you as they do, or so it seems. You have not only separated from a partner and a lover, but also a best friend. Whether the feelings and thoughts make you believe that better and more compatible would ever come along, that you will never be happy without them, letting go is the answer.

Letting go is a personal necessity. Above all, what matters at this time is your own wellbeing and freedom. Attachment is an energetic chain. The feelings and emotions experienced after separation only serve to create an unhealthy connection. The process of letting go benefits both partners. This is another form in which love can be expressed. Heartbreak provides a space in which to heal, so other energies can be restored. As one heals, the other heals too. The connection is selfless. One of the twin flames has to heal first. Taking responsibility is also an act of love for another. The special connection and love remain. Yet, letting go is the only answer if only temporarily. The legacy the relationship leaves behind is an inner connection that had never been touched before. It is a place from which to build the person that one wants to be. Nothing is lost. Only the forms have changed. Life will never be the same again. Honour love, do celebrate their existence, the time spent together; keep loving. Love continues being the vehicle to heal. Shadow work has taken you to a darker room where truth and love is found.

Both tradition and society teach that love relates to possession; to a life of togetherness. This is the tyranny of the fear of being alone and probably one of the reasons to seek love in the first place. However uncomfortable it might feel, being alone is another opportunity to get to know the self. The soul is a gypsy in love that wants to travel, go on an adventure of self-discovery and in most cases, it is a path that needs to be walked alone. One does not necessarily have to travel alone, but adventure sometimes leads to darker periods. The fact that one has not yet found a companion or might have separated from one is not a reason to stop moving, to stop traveling, however heart breaking the separation is. The most important relationship is the one you have with yourself. Social conditioning as to what life is meant to be or not, only removes creativity and curiosity from a human being, deterring infinite possibilities to create better worlds. At this point, one has no choice but to continue walking alone. Keep walking. There are healthy steps to better places.

Attachment does not allow healing. We are here to learn love, to heal, to create. Letting go of whom you most love is one true expression of unconditional love, a certain way to reconnect with the soul. It is a paradox. Perhaps it does not make sense initially, but in time the rewards will be obvious. The reunion will never occur until one has mastered the art of letting go. It is also essential that the other person let's go too. The fact that the runner goes away does not necessarily mean that they let go at all. It is even possible that they are even more attached than their partner. The energy and the connection are still needed. It is their selfish nature, the energetic space where they are now. The more energy they use to escape, the stronger the connection becomes even when there is no physical contact. They might appear to have made the decision. It is possible that they used all the strength they had left to do so, but the runner is the one that suffers most. The twin flame runner runs away from love to break their own heart. They are not running away from you; they are running away from themselves. Everything is a paradox.

Both parties must let go in order to make the reunion possible. It is the reason why one person alone cannot attract another regardless of what they do or how proficient they might be in manifesting. The twin is a soul, a free spirit, and anything one can humanly attempt to attract them might not necessarily work if only one of them holds that intention. A twin flame does not appear to everyone, and if he or she does in this lifetime, perhaps another twenty years will pass by before reuniting. Letting go is also an act of love, and perhaps, only perhaps, you are here, I am here, we are here only to learn to let go. Letting go is freedom, but also an undeniable part of life. Where there is freedom, there is love. It is then that one can achieve anything and everything. Keep loving, keep trusting and be; just be. Everything appears at the right time. The right time is often a matter of choice.

Separating From the Twin Flame.

Relationships end. It is a fact of life. The end is heart breaking for the majority of people. The sense of estrangement is usually shocking. There are of course break ups that are liberating. Either way, heartbreak could be one of the best things that could happen to people, putting aside the initial emotional distress. While the immediate emotional state may be devastating, the space produced by the separation serves the purpose of healing and personal growth. Every situation, however negative, hides opportunities and answers to existential dilemmas. In love is the space everyone wants to be. There are different ways to get there.

Meeting with your twin flame brings a mixed feeling of ecstasy and relief. Life is finally coming with a break, a moment to breathe. The break is not really needed, as in love is a state of being to which one can get to alone, but the adventure is more entertaining with the love and the complicity of a partner. There are periods in life in which it is necessary to be alone in order to grow. Lack of growth during the relationship equals a sense of stagnation. Healthy and creative energies are not flowing, which in turn invites to seek new spaces in which someone feels and lives different opportunities.

Whether the growth required is personal or professional achievement and circumstances might be varied, a time of solitude is necessary in a demanding world. Achieving a stronger sense of self, allows an opportunity to establish a deeper, magnetic connection with a romantic partner. It is also possible that in times of hardship a relationship begins. There are no rules. The possibility that throughout life one has not yet managed to meet a romantic partner or someone that fully understands is high, thus, the relief, the sensation of having been given a break. Any form of love allows to view life from a more colourful and vibrant perspective. Being in love is magic.

The element of friendship in the twin flame connection comes along with a sense of freedom. It is a creative and expansive space. In this space one feels liberated, there is no longer the impression that they have to hide or mask authenticity or cover up any flaws. Imperfections are as loved as good qualities are. Flaws or imperfections are often product of a competitive society that demands perfection in every aspect from everyone. For the twin flame expressing with ease gifts, talents or flaws means being authentic. It inspires to express the best in us. He or she is the person one has spent a lifetime waiting for, to live the memory of something never experienced, but which is vibrantly alive within the emotional body. In a more conscious world, in the sense that people followed their intuition, expressing their true essence, words and desires openly, everyone would be aware of the next step to come, what decision to make. Meeting the twin flame feels as if reliving a memory or a dream, only that this time their   presence   is   physical,   real.

Reminiscence creates an energetic map, which guides people through life in search of such evocative love. It is the reunion with the twin flame. Unfortunately, many people give up on their memories and dreams, to fall for the prevailing idea to settle for a safe life. A safe life is an illusion, one of the legacies of patriarchy, a taught paradigm. The crushing feeling of incompleteness. There is no safety in safe. It takes courage, not only to manifest a lover, but to seek and achieve a dream life. Settling for a safe life or renouncing to a dream does not remove the feeling, the hope of love, but it might lead to a deeper sense of dissatisfaction. This person becomes a seeker, and he or she won't stop until they the feeling becomes a reality.

The safety referred to in this chapter refers to love. Of course that it is wise to find safe spaces and a life of abundance that permits to meet everyone's needs. In this case, safety could be sought for several reasons: fear of love, loneliness, fear of abandonment, low self-esteem or the belief that one does not deserve or won't be able to find what they want. Each of these reasons have different roots, as well as solutions that can be reached with shadow work. Often the source of trauma have faded. Not being able to identify the source of trauma makes shadow work more difficult initially. The root is hidden in the small details. They are repetitive, as they are exhausting.

Trauma could have its origins in subtle events. To experience the cold response of a mother at a young age, or even during adolescence is likely to cause trauma on her daughter. The daughter's response to love and relationships could vary depending on her ability to process and deal with rejection. For her, love may never be safe, seeking partners she does not have to fully give her heart to. The caretaker is unavailable and neglectful. This rationale leads to multiple partners, not because she is interested in a variety of lovers, but due to the fact that as soon as she perceives more love that she is prepared to give, she will shut down emotionally and run away. Non-attachment is safe for her. Eventually she will meet someone that she falls in love with. The fate of the relationship might be the same. In this case, this person sabotages the relationship from the beginning consciously. Everything is a barrier to love. Emotional shut down and termination is the result. Twin flame or not, we have a runner. Such individual feels that they are not good enough, need constant attention and confirmation, but from a safe distance. The same emotional distance kept by her mother. The fact that they can continue turning to their mothers when convenient has another effect on relationships. This traumatic episode could take place when the girl is 5 or 17 years old. It is the moment the daughter realises that there is no one to turn to. She feels lonely, depressed and unprotected. In her life, she could conduct herself confidently. There is no reason for anyone to remain reproducing traumas of the past, but deep inside, a sense that she is not good enough lingers, which in turn will require the attention of others, usually the opposite sex to try and fill the void. They know that love is near and available. In order to keep a safe distance, they do not always have to return to the same partner. To avoid rejection, they avoid others.

Fear of abandonment has a damaging effect, not only in relationships, but on the person functioning under its spell. As everyone else, they do want to love and be loved. However, a series of automatisms is developed in order to suppress all emotion, and might not be willing to take on shadow work or any other type of personal development course. With each break up, they hurt themselves and others, but the response is too cold to feel heartbreak. Heartbreak in this people is unavoidable. Eventually they meet someone who will indeed leave them, someone they can actually love. The feeling of abandonment increases. Paradoxically, people who experience fear of abandonment are the most romantic of all, but they do not let it be seen. It is a cold, distant character, and if not fully, they do tend to develop narcissistic traits and behaviour. Love is not safe, and yet, love is all they seek.

When this type of individual feels an intense love for another in a relationship, they do tend to numb their feelings. It is also possible that they sabotage the relationship from the beginning, causing a distorted reality that is distressing and weakening to both, but that is particularly disturbing to their partner, as they see no reason for such behaviour. Eventually they will leave the relationship with an insulting coldness. This is an individual that hurts deeply, but does not know or does not want to deal with their emotions, moving from passionate to dispassionate in a matter of seconds. Feelings of inadequacy appear when they are alone. Sometimes it is a matter of minutes to reach this state.

The concept of an inexplicable memory or dream of a person never met can be explained from the perspective that everything is here and now. How this memory sets in someone's emotional field also varies, and for the purpose of this book is irrelevant. An example is someone who appears in a dream repeatedly. When the dream is premonitory, the dreamer recognises the energy of the dream, and in this case, not only the memory is created, but there is also the image of a lover who is about to enter and change the course of life. The memory could be as simple as an energy that has been present since childhood.

Understanding the purpose of the memory is crucial to manifest a fulfilling life. There are three elements that come into play: time, space and energy. Everything that has ever existed, everything that there is and everything that there will ever exist is here and now. With this understanding, one can remember the future, as if it had already happened. To fully comprehend this concept, and how it works, one has to connect with their intuition, as well as creating a new belief. An intellectual understanding might not suffice, as it escapes reason or the logic of what is taught by the established education system and the set of standard beliefs, lacking the tangibility that can be prove its existence and authenticity. It is one of the unexplainable wonders   in   life.

Many people will not meet their twin flame for this reason; lack of belief, and the courage or patience to remain alone while seeking for what they want. In order to meet the twin flame, the adventure is necessary. It is looking actively, not for the physical person, but for healing and a higher state of consciousness through connecting with their inner source. The twin flame appears when belief, trust and hope beat vibrant in one's heart, not in the mind.

In a world where is hard to trust anyone else, the encounter with a friend feels like Nirvana. It is unfortunate that the human being relies on others to reach it. The journey to Nirvana can and has to be done alone. However, being surrounded by people moving towards the same destination is a blessing, as a healthy exchange helps to build community and expansion through and with others. While accepting who we are is an exercise of honesty that one has to face alone, there is no reason why anyone has to go through the process completely alone. If not among friends, likeminded people can be found within the community. If in need of assistance, one might want to hire the services of a professional in order to gain knowledge and a sense of direction. At any stage in life being surrounded by healthy and creative people can and will determine one's personal development. Healthy is understood, as people doing their best to reach or maintain a sense of inner peace, as well as having the same approach with others. Everyone is influenced either positively or negatively by the company we keep. It is important to choose wisely. Being in a romantic relationship brings a different energy to one's environment, as well as comfort, support and encouragement. However, having in mind that we are responsible for finding our own answers is a healthy step to find them. For as long as answers are sought in or from others, answers might be evasive.

Friendship with a twin flame is a lifetime connection, even when paths separate. Both remain loyal to the idea, the feeling. They might never want to meet again, but love remains behind a sheltered heart. The physical end of friendship takes over the mind. Emptiness follows. It is a desolate space to be, which might create the belief that it will never be possible to find someone else with whom we may create a similar or better feeling. This is another belief with no basis to exist other than in the mind, although understandable considering the depletion of vital energy at this stage. A period to familiarise with this new phase is needed. The emotional neediness due to attachment opposed to the physical absence of a lover brings a feeling of rejection, as well as self-rejection. Being rejected by a lover causes self-rejection as a means to maintain the connection. It is unhealthy validation, but one that unconsciously preserves the complicity they couple had. In both, presence and absence, the twin flame continues indicating the way. The feeling could remain for years, turning someone's emotional space into a desert, where no other than the love who got away is accepted. A compassionate view of heartbreak and its immediate consequences allows understanding this emotional reasoning. The sense of loss remains, but also an opportunity to transcend this state of being. When the heart breaks, the ex-lover is so far the only physical reference of love, friendship and understanding. This is how a heart closes to love and life, a way to create another energetic prison. Self-imprisonment is fear of love, fear of experiencing life to the full. Once someone has been hurt it is safe to close the door to love. Some people never recover. They might never let love in again. Responding to a break up in a healthy and creative manner opens an array of possibilities, as well as providing energetic resources for personal growth. There is life after the twin flame, as there is love after love. In other words, love is an act of rebellion.

The end of the relationship is not the end of friendship. It only appears to be so. There are a few facts that might be escaping one's perception due to their emotional state. Being deprived of love after a relationship opens a wound that runs deep to the source of trauma reliving it. Heartbreak is essential in order to heal. As essential as the response to it. Heartbreak allows to get in touch with one's feelings; feelings that otherwise one might have never dared to experience. The first step is acceptance.

From here on, one continues being as authentic as hurt allows. Authenticity is not a projection to be shown only to a romantic partner. It is an act of self-expression to yourself, then the world. The fact that the twin flame abandons the boat indicates that you are now ready to sail alone. They would not want, nor expect less from you. What the twin flame would like from you is to live. To live a life that is full, so as to make the best of every opportunity has a lot to do with the separation. Take stock of your life and consider how you lived your life so far. It might have been lacking in personal ambition in terms of growth, creativity and passion for who you are. The presence of the twin flame acts as a spark that lightens up life, with the consequent plans and desires for the future. If all intention remains talk, and plans are daily postponed for a better future, your partner might see that your creative energy remains stagnant, perhaps due to their presence. Creativity works as a glue in relationships, while passivity or procrastination are signs that one still fears to show up in their own life. The same applies to them. The twin flame is perhaps too magnetic delaying any form of achievement, both personally and as a couple. The separation should be reason enough to ignite a fire within, which allows the individual to move with more determination. Heartbreak, sadness or depression prolongs a life not lived. A separation may require a period of solace and rest in order to regain energy, but it is not a lifetime plan. The mourning has to end. One has to find that spark within, this time with a greater purpose. The twin flame has already caused you to show your magic. Use it. It is always there. Perhaps an individual delayed expressing authenticity until the right person appeared, but once the process has started, there is no reason to withdraw, nor to hide. The way to see and perceive whether the steps taken from then on are the appropriate ones is by interpreting the energy that moves through the body. Actions bring feelings that affect and manifest different states of being. Uncompromising authenticity is a source of vital energy. If it feels good, it is the right step. Do what makes you happy.

The full expression of the self cannot be devoted to one person only, but to the entire world. What we look for is the universal; universal and unconditional love, therefore one continues expressing themselves without fear. By expressing who we are to the world, the need to hide ends. Practice becomes habits. Practice yourself in different ways. There is nothing to hide. Secrets are not so secret, and while someone might be under the impression that they are somehow special and different, everyone else is also unique, and likely to be struggling with similar issues. Practice authenticity. It grows on you. When you speak your truth, people whose position in your life is ambivalent do disappear, leaving room for others from whom you will receive friendship, support and acceptance.

In order to express authenticity it is crucial to differentiate between the expression of the soul, and that of the ego. The soul speaks in a language that allows vulnerability, but also energy, love, joy and passion. While ego somehow bestows a person with a certain degree of functionality, it also leads individuals to dead ends and struggles. Separating is an excellent opportunity to distance the self from the dictate of ego. Ego's resistance creates separation, from the self, then from others. It is a personal choice to continue allowing ego to rule your life, or to allow a path of responsibility, fun and humbleness. Three personal and healthy characteristics that the ego does not know   of.

The end of physical friendship is perhaps the most devastating aspect after the separation. The dialogue is abruptly interrupted. One can continue confiding in others, but at this moment in time it might not be possible to reach the same degree of trust or understanding. The level of understanding that a twin flame offers cannot be reached by everyone. Thus, sadness and feelings of abandonment grow deeper. The human tendency to emotionally coil after experiences of loss or separation is not limited to attachment. People are the first ones to underestimate themselves. As a consequence, apathy follows. What most people would do for others, they would never do for themselves. Someone would make incredible efforts to find a recipe, shop for ingredients, allocate time and space, clear and clean the house, organise invitations, choose the right people for a home meal, but hardly would they ever treat themselves in the same way. If friends treated us as we treat ourselves, we would drop them like a ton of bricks without hesitation. Separation from a romantic relationships brings both, the time and the opportunity to step up and truly begin to take care of ourselves.

Accepting that the current situation cannot be changed, one becomes aware that it is the perfect time to build a relationship with the self. It is never soon enough to accept this fact. The relationship with the self is the most important relationship of all. One must become their own best friend. If in doubt where to begin, ask yourself what you need. Ask, but do not answer your own questions. Allow silence to take over. The answers will come. You already know what you need. This is the beginning of a better relationship with yourself. A door is open to explore intimacy with the self. Silence is a step forward. To answer a question immediately does not vary from the usual inner conversations that continually take place in the mind. It is the common pattern followed by most people, finding immediate, logical answers to questions that often are not responded to with action. Being your best friend requires a proactive approach. Conversations between people often lack space for silence, feeling and reflection, as if it was imperative to contribute further to the noise of the world. Intimacy, an essential element in the relationship with the self, demands also the exploration of silence. Silence is an underestimated tool containing multiple and healthy answers to daily problems. The reason not to answer immediately are several. Ego is always ready to introduce a clever strategy that does not lead to successful outcomes in matters concerning the spiritual and personal growth. Ego's response is immediate, but only validates what is known. Heartbreak to ego is a flag of sorrows seeking attention. One also lacks vital energy or motivation. It is a matter of taking small steps. Once the question has been raised, the answers will appear as they are needed. Silence is a form of self-reflection. There is an intuitive energy and source of wisdom that could provide a solution to every problem one may have. If these answers do not appear more often it is because human beings continue reproducing the noise of the world in inner conversations. As answers appear, body, mind and spirit become accustomed to their energy, thus preparing the self to allow a healthier and more proactive response in practical terms.

At some point in life, one has to realise that the best tool and the best vehicle for transformation and success is the self. The ex-partner is no longer available to offer support. It is essential that we remove the idea of another person as the saviour. The best friend one could ever have is within. Become the person to whom you will be excited to answer the phone or spend time with. Would you date yourself at this moment in time? This is a question that does not even need an answer. Although on the negative scale as it is connected to trauma, pain and suffering, this is knowing. How the response resonates within your being is symptomatic of which direction you should take from now on. For as long as answers are sought outside, isolation and a state of lack remain. You are the answer. Perhaps you have been waiting too long to put it into practice.

An indicative that shadow work needs to be done alone is when the person who has been abandoned is meeting again with the same outcome. It might be a pattern. There are people who adapt to their partners in every relationship. They are most flexible, and for a period, this is a quality that it is admired and appreciated by others. Love is flexible. This type of behaviour could be interpreted as an excess of love. It is in many ways unconditional. The element to look for is, if this is a natural pattern of behaviour or an excessive need for love. It is possible that this individual is also affected by fear of abandonment, having met their match. Getting comfortable with being alone, not only is an attractive feature, it contributes to build self-esteem and confidence, but also it allows the patience to wait for the right person. There is a thin line between fear of abandonment and fear of being alone. The needy energy interferes with love, and while it is not for them to take responsibility for their partner's actions it denotes weakness, which in turn affects confidence. As the relationship develops, flexibility gives their partner a carte blanche to do anything they wish, knowing that they will be accepted and forgiven unconditionally. It deteriorates inner strength, as one has given control in the relationship to their partner.

However amazing the relationship with a twin flame has been, what makes an individual feel alive and liberated is not entirely the physical contact, but the fact that authenticity comes natural. One does not need a twin flame or a lover to do so. Authenticity can be shown anytime. The person becomes the limitation when there is a belief that their deepest emotions require the perfect container.

Shutting down is a natural reaction after a separation, so as to preserve everything that is beautiful and good in us, something that one may believe that it can only be offered to their lover. The wound needs time to heal. This is caused by an understandable sense of loyalty towards the other person. Love still beats in the heart. This kind of loyalty must end and be focused towards the self. One might not be willing to offer love or physical contact to anyone other than the twin flame, but to save the best of yourself for a lover now gone and whom may never return is madness. It is a certain way to wither and destroy the best qualities in a person. There is no loyalty in someone leaving the relationship for any of the reasons described in this book. Of course, it does not include abusive relationships. In case of abuse, leaving is the best option. Loyalty begins with the self, and the ex-lover by leaving has already taking this step. Loyalty should not be used as an excuse for self-rejection.

Consciously censoring one's true expression, one recedes into a state of seclusion in which the soul feels incarcerated. Anyone would react to this kind of censorship if someone else attempted to impose it upon them. Freedom is an act of rebellion. The inner revolution that leads to complete independence from the tyranny of ego goes through acts of self-expression that make an individual feel alive. Live as if love was already here. True friendship with the self is to honour yourself by bringing your life to the best state possible. You may honour the memory of a past lover, but neglecting yourself by living in a permanent and passionless state of lack causes a little death while still alive. It is not a life, but self-punishment. The cruellest form of self-imprisonment is to continue following the limiting instructions that others have given us throughout life, especially parents. Do not accept from yourself what you would not accept from others. As with everything else, one becomes what they practise. Love is also a practice. Making a cup of tea a ritual to treat yourself is love. Buy yourself flowers. Sit down to eat calmly. All this is love. Practising self-denial prevents love for as long as it continues. Love is magnetic instead. Healthy and positive choices are obvious. The time to make those choices is now.

The soul is always safe. No one can damage it. To believe that a soul can be damaged or fragmented is another intrusion by social conditioning in the human psyche, this time, an infantile over embellishment of a fairy tale. You do not owe your live to a past lover, but to yourself, to the world and the universe. The relationship with the twin flame has already led to find an authentic expression. Now it is time to continue using through creativity and self-love. The kind of creativity that leads to build a reality that meets your needs and facilitates personal expansion. These are the elements that made you attractive to another in the first instance. Closing to the world instead, deters all chances to find true love. If the separation is recent, it is possible that someone does not feel, nor needs or wants to meet someone else, but as life continues, it is only natural to open up to the possibility. You never know what tomorrow will bring to your door. Be ready.

As a relationship ends, someone may think that a solitary period or low moods may be a temporary phase. Accepting what is true today should serve as an excuse to remain in such state permanently. Too many people indulge in this state of being once love is gone and proceed to create a chapter of a self-mythological creature that lives in pain and endless suffering. It is human condition to celebrate defeats, while neglecting our victories. A low mood, depression and even heartbreak can at times and depending on the individual become a door to immediate gratification, leading to numerous excuses and to unhealthy habits. This kind of belief is also a practice, which if prolonged in time may never allow happiness, abundance or love. One cannot decide the length of time that a temporary low mood may last, but it can determine to take positive and healthy steps towards a better future from the first day, always considering their levels of energy, immediate commitments and possibilities. A healthy step is to look at what possibilities one may have, and not to look at it as limitations. The possibility begins where the limitation ends. Focusing on the limitation, it becomes permanent. Someone might be extremely talented at a craft, art or in communicating skills, but have heard from an early age to take responsibility and choose a more serious or normal line of work. This becomes a limitation. At a certain age, one has the choice to rebel and follow their heart by practising more of what they are good at. To continue listening to what they always heard is now a self-imposed limitation, and it denies creativity and true self-expression. If we are to live a fantasy, why not live one that is full of love? Most limitations only live in the mind. It is extraordinary what a person can achieve once they set their minds to it. It is a matter of perspective, as well as belief. Belief also comes with new practices, by undertaking on different activities and alternative responses to similar situations, but above all, the emotional responses given to stimuli.

Through a healthy friendship with the self, one creates opportunities to open once again to love, but before this point is reached, let go also of the idea of how and what it should be. Simply allow it. This is another step towards the reunion with the twin flame. Until then, make the most of it.

Fear of Love

Fear of love is a paradox affecting almost every human being. It is not easy to perceive, but it is a phenomena easy to understand once the reasons are known. Its complexity lies hidden in the fact that everyone is looking for love, to love and be loved. It does not make sense that someone is afraid of what they look for. Everything in life is a paradox. The term 'fear of love' can be misleading. It is not that people fear love, but the hurt that may come in a relationship once personal defences and boundaries have been dropped. Love cannot be expressed, nor received without a certain degree of vulnerability. The downside of vulnerability is that it cannot prevent hurt. Hurt might to come intentionally.

The signs are fairly visible and can affect both partners in the relationship. Someone would react disproportionately to signs of affection, setting a distance that is considered safe. At this point one of the partners begins to show signs of disaffection and avoidance if only temporarily. Anyone who suffered physical abuse in childhood would feel tense at any physical contact even if this is most loving. It is worth pointing out that physical or sexual abuse in childhood can be punctual, not the norm, but that it would leave an energetic imprint that can set off triggers at any point in life. It is usual among victims of sexual abuse to block such episodes and even to bury entire years of their lives in order to suppress any recollection of the events. In both cases, whether a person has experienced one or the other, physical contact may represent a challenge in the intimate relationship of a couple.

For these people exploring intimacy with a partner becomes an issue, as they are not used to the most gentle touch from another person having grown accustomed to a more violent or abusive contact. It does feel unfamiliar, even threatening. It is distrust of the unknown. It is natural in people who have suffered abuse to seek abusive relationships. They might not like it, but they do know how to cope with it. The message to step into the unknown is common among the spiritual community and widely spread. However, there is not much explanation of what the unknown is, leaving it open to interpretation that often leads to impossibility, as it is a concept that it is not clearly defined, and yet, it is clear and obvious. In this regard, to enter the unknown is to surrender to vulnerability, so as to allow the loving touch of the partner. The unknown would be, those feelings and emotions perceived at receiving gentle and loving physical contact, and by allowing it to happen to feel a new sensation, in order to get used to it. It is one of the most important parts a couple can do in shadow work. For an abuse survivor, such contact is unfamiliar and perhaps unsettling. It is an instinctual reaction for reasons they might ignore. They will be the first ones to be surprised at their reactions, although it is possible that they do keep it in silence, learning to avoid contact. The repercussions in the relationship could be disastrous, if not dealt with effectively. While it is natural for a couple to have intimate and sexual contact during a relationship, their level of intimacy might only touch the surface. Fear of intimacy in itself is a plague affecting most of the population in a society that over-sexualises everything, excluding the more sensual and deeper senses of the human being. Intimacy is a platform from which humanity could find a great sense of relief, as well as to enable to recapture that essence of what being human is. There is a large number of people, both men and women who react to triggers due to past relationships, which are not considered abusive, but that do contain all the elements of an abusive relationship and even sexual abuse. There is still much to learn about consent or simply respect in society; two necessary steps in order to find love.

Fear of love does not require undergoing extreme experiences, such as physical or sexual abuse to be present in psyche and body. The explanation is simpler. All children are born in love. For a period of time children continue experiencing such blessed state. As time goes by children grow more conscious, self-aware and more aware of the ways of the world. Some experiences growing up can be challenging and traumatic causing a damaging effect that causes separating from love. A child learns to fear their parents, their beliefs, their way of living and behaviours. Often the adult environment does not match the needs or the vibrational state of a child. None of these episodes necessarily involve deliberate malice. In this way everybody becomes familiar with fear befalling more receptive to it. It is also as simple as adopting their parent's fears. Money problems, disagreements or negative experiences with others affect the growth of a child. A child listens, being an energetic sponge and learning behavioural models from close relatives. No matter how good a parent is, a child always develops a trauma. Eventually what they see daily becomes the truth. The child separates from their true potential, renouncing to their talents and gifts by mimicking behaviour and following the beliefs of their role models. The perception is that the natural instincts and wisdom of the child does not match the ways of the world and in order to function, wisdom and vision are compromised, in an attempt to recreate a person that fits within the perceived normality. Some of these episodes could be an alarming warning coming from a parent that is trying to prevent harm in their children, which to the child may come as a shock. At that age, children have not built barriers to filter adequately the nature of the information that is received, as it is biased. Defence mechanisms develop to hide the innate abilities of the child, including love. The older they get, the more fear is adopted in people's psyche and behaviour. Slowly one becomes unaccustomed to love. It is a natural process, which often cannot be blamed on a parent.

The fear of a parent does not have to relate to a terrifying scenario. Fear is presented to all of us in the form of boundaries and limitations. How parents discipline their children also play an important part. Depending on who those parents are, there is also a sense of abandonment or lack of love. For one, parents cannot be constantly paying attention to the children. Abandonment can be as simple as the first day of nursery school or the birth of a new sibling needing more care and attention. Many parents cannot express love to their children because they grew up in a home in which love was not expressed openly. Acting distant and unemotional to the needs of their children, the child learns to accept this type of behaviour, which later on in life, and once in a committed relationship would set all the alarms off. There is the kind of parent who should never be allowed to go anywhere near a child. Not their own, nor any other child.

Some parents enter parenthood accidentally due to unwanted pregnancies. There are numerous cases in which one or even both parents remove themselves from the map creating a feeling of abandonment. At the same time, someone who does not want children accepts the new reality and could even become a good parent. Many people rise up to the challenges of life gaining in maturity, as well as accepting responsibility when a child is born. However, an overlooked fact is that children begin to absorb information energetically in the womb. The reaction of a person before witnessing the birth of their child might still be loaded with feelings of rejection, which inevitably reaches the foetus. Everything is energy, being children the most receptive to the actions, thoughts and feelings of their environment. A child may already be born fearing love. In this case, children learn to live in a loveless reality and even when they are loved, the feeling of being unwanted and underserving might last a lifetime. The storm of feelings and emotions to which a child is exposed due to the unconscious acts of their parents during the pregnancy creates an energy absorbed by the child. The struggle does not end there, even when both parents remain. Parents deliberately use these experiences against each other, often using the child against each other without consideration for their children in order to satisfy their own selfish needs. Some of these acts could be unconscious, but many are deliberate, as well as egotistic. It could be one of the parents who does not feel loved by their partner. Numerous relationships are barely glued together and only functioning due to the responsibility they have towards the child. An unwanted pregnancy often creates distrust, a sense of possession. However much a parent loves their new born, when they remain in the relationship to support their children, it is still possible that they hold a grudge.

Parenthood changes someone's life drastically, often thwarting someone's dreams of expansion and freedom.

For the child there is not a parallel or supporting education giving especial emphasis to love, freedom nor happiness, as the focus is on the mundane, the prosaic trivialities of their environment, causing an imbalance between what is important and what is not in the development of a human being. Reality takes over. Their true nature comes second. Thus, love becomes unimportant, unfamiliar.

The majority of twin flame runners fit one, if not all of the descriptions written above. Feelings of rejection or feeling unloved may still be unconscious even when someone aware of the significant events in their life, or the elements that contributed to shape their character, personality and behaviour. Any relationship worth mentioning or considered is born out of love. When the appearance of a first love, a person begins to open their heart to multiple possibilities, reaching out to memories of dreams and a world that finally reflects the never forgotten portrait of perfect love. Love is perfection in any form. Relationships are fertile grounds where dreams of childhood combined with personal abilities allow dreams once again to blossom. As people fall in love, the honeymoon period temporarily removes all obstacles to love. Love's energy reawakens. Everything is possible.

In time, learned behaviour is unavoidable. We become what we practise. In all relationships one of the partners is more affectionate than the other. The partner that grew up in an environment where love was not expressed openly is more prone to distrust. Intentions are questioned even if not expressed to their partner. One lives under the impression that fear and doubt may not be the appropriate step to take. Personal shadows are overlooked, as what one wants and expects to receive is love. Without an intimate debate on such issues, separation from love fills the space. Trust issues begin to take a toll on the relationship. Unspoken truths may be the beginning of heartbreak and separation. Heartbreak is already within, as it has been experienced during childhood. It is familiar. Being overly affectionate to this type of lover will certainly send them into a defensive position. The issues that are introduced internally might not be conscious. If not dealt with, the debate is internal and in a solitary place where their lover can neither enter, nor offer support. Even though constant reassurance of love is sought and needed, there are elements that someone might not be able to rationalise. It is real? Can it be real? In this new emotional state, love is on trial and bound to be sentenced to exile, as the energy that is fed is doubt and fear. At the same time, this person is in love, feeling raw and vulnerable, which invite the energies of memories perhaps forgotten, but that suggest hurt.

When someone is affected by fear of love, they might begin relationships with people they cannot fully fall in love with. They would be attracted to parts of their partners, but immediately will find fault, which in turn leads to more reasons, in this case excuses to end relationships. In the quest for love, these individuals would move from relationship to relationship without commitment, not any intention to remain. Relationships are temporary. Each of these relationship evokes past feelings and emotions, as well as a loveless reality that supports the belief that love is neither real, not possible. Often these relationships begin due to lust or infatuation. Often the feeling of love is not recognised or admitted. It is not that they are not capable of living, nor that they do not wish to find a loving and lasting relationship, but that life experiences and relationships proved to be impossible. In such acute cases, these individuals are runners; nomads that move from place to place seeking the Holy Grail. They do find romanticism in the discomfort of the adventure. Their lives become a vehicle to express their tortured self-mythology. From this perspective, these individual would find easier to engage in temporary or even casual relationships in order to remain safe. They know that choosing partners to whom they cannot feel attached to make their decision to leave much easier when the call comes. If the twin flame is driven by this powerful energy, once the meeting occurs and the relationship begins, they would be most passionate, surrendering to the love. The urge to leave becomes dormant. Finally they found home.

It might not be too long before they feel the call of freedom and detachment again. When this happens, they will sabotage the relationship. Through experience they have become masters of sabotage to everything and everyone that reflects love. Love is not a safe place for them. How sabotage occurs is obvious to both partners. It is their way to ask for the end of the relationship. One does not necessarily need to stop loving another to end the relationship. The need for what they consider freedom is a powerful force. This is fear of love at its worse. There is nothing one can do to stop them from leaving, even if when they do, they break their own hearts. In such cases, the return of the twin flame might never take place. The paradox is that as what they fear most is being abandoned, they would take this step themselves. The irony is that the deprive themselves of what they want by leaving it. Somehow ending the relationship gives people a certain feeling of power and false security, as they are the decision makers. It is customary for them to share with others that they always ended their relationships. However powerful it makes them feel, in time it will turn against them. While they may believe that they hold a power of some sorts, the effect is the opposite. It weakens their emotional body making every new relationship more difficult. It is a narcissistic behaviour that can only worsen coiled in the ways of their ego. The twin flame relationship opens a new possibility to heal these shadows, so as to live a happy and fulfilling life. If they leave, the relationship with their twin flame will cast a shadow on other relationships to come. Being in a relationship with this kind of person drains energy from their partner. The attempts to end are followed by reconciliation and then again another break up to resume the relationship once again until the situation is untenable. It depletes the energy of their partners. It is a constant call for attention, to feel loved and sought after. The psychological and emotional wounds left in their partners after the relationship is over equal the symptoms of someone who has been in an abusive relationship. It could be a long road to recovery.

A practical example of this type of personality and how the cause chaos within the relationship is their proneness to be angry at their partners by manipulating situations without logical reasons. This kind of individual conceals multiple traps around their personal space using them as triggers to undermine the emotional state of their partner, which in turn cause insecurity and has an incredibly negative on their self-esteem. This act might be unconscious, but it is often only targeted at their partners, while they continue having a jovial and energised attitude among others. They need to have control of all situations at all times, and in the event that they allow room for improvisation, their partners will suffered their rage if anything went wrong. They also tend to have short lived relationships, are unfaithful or have multiple lovers at the same time in non-committed relationships. Paradoxically, they do tend to have the warmest hearts, and be the kindest people.

The relationship becomes an emotional storm that requires perspective and abundance of patience, as it escapes all logic. The runner just expressed their undying love for their lover. They feel it, and they mean it. Yet, they feel compelled to run away. It is a time for love, compassion and understanding, although it might turn out to be a near impossible exercise. At this stage everything points out to the end of the relationship. The possibility of a positive outcome is always present. However, the relationship becomes a mine field full of traps that trigger the runner, what might provoke further reactions from both. When there is no logic, keeping a distance allows to find solutions. A reaction from one of the lovers that is followed by another reaction leads to arguments or accusations or both.

An appropriate response to such a situation would be non-reactive, to remain calm and let the storm pass. Before such response, the runner is rendered powerless, as they are met with love and understanding. Peace and love follows. But be aware that ego is always lurking to say the final word. This scenario is a portrait an extreme situation that can go wrong any time. One of the partners may become accustomed to get away with anything and continue finding opportunities to run and hide. One of the purposes of this book is to find solutions before reaching to this point. In his book 'An Uncommon Bond' Jeff Foster suggests that the first thing to ask someone before starting a relationship is if they are prepared to do shadow work. Shadow work allows to unveil and deal with all these issues as they appear, with love, patience and awareness. Awareness of any situation opens space for compassion and understanding so as to add the tools and time needed. It might not sound like the most attractive activity to do in a relationship, especially at the beginning, but situations would be presented in which either partner may introduce the idea. The alternative may well be a farewell.

The twin flame relationship might be the first time in which both lovers truly mean to give and receive love. While it might not make sense, it is easy for two lovers with such an amazing connection to be in love, as well as rejecting each other. Feelings and emotions run high and deep. Demons and fears are having a wild energetic feast. The experience could turn out to be so daunting that the relationship might have to end in order to survive it. It is often the case that both people realise this fact and agree on a separation even when they are still in love.

Twin flames or not, anyone involved in a relationship affected by fear of love would eventually show the opposite of what they claim to feel. It does not make sense to them either. It is an uncontrollable reaction to an overwhelming emotion. It is not that they cannot love. They do. It is the inner child in a reactive mode manipulating their lover with the same controlling attitude their parents showed towards them. The problem is that they refuse to accept a part of the self that is clearly creating mayhem in their lives. It becomes the true false nature, which they will defend at all cost. It is also the inability to allow emotions to run their natural course.

The answer to this problem, as well as the solution lies with the inner child in the shadows. Awareness is the first step. Without awareness, these episodes remain unconscious, causing further damage to the relationship and the self. What we do to others, we do to ourselves. Equally important is the fact that what we do to ourselves, we do to others.

Awareness opens the door that leads to the source of the problem, allowing anyone to be a witness to their own actions. When an individual is aware of the vicissitudes of their own process and where they may be triggered, through self-acceptance they can prevent reactive behaviour avoiding blame and other self-inflicted emotions such as guilt or shame. The relationship grows in emotional intelligence, providing opportunities to create safe spaces for deeper and intimate conversations. If this stage is reached, the chances to create a healthy and strong relationship increase dramatically, as each step opens one's heart to their partner, thus experiencing kinder emotions. To open one's heart is to allow ourselves to love others.

Let's return to the beginning. The portrait of a relationship described in this chapter could create a terrifying impression in the reader. It is not necessary to reach this stage in a relationship. This is the reason why people write or read books and different publications, to raise awareness on different issues where experience is used to identify all the elements and situations that offer guidance. Investing in personal development might be an expensive business, but it is as necessary as investing in education. To live a loveless life due to unconscious beliefs is even more expensive. The investment at this point is in love. In love anyone can find what is needed for a successful relationship. Love is a space where miracles do happen.

At recognising any of the signs examined in this chapter, and whether it is part of your personal process or is coming from your partner, pause and reflect. It is time to engage in an intimate conversation, to resort to the endless resources of emotional intelligence. In order to access the hidden reserves contained within someone's heart, one must first do an exercise of honesty and admit that this is where they are at the present moment. Vulnerability also opens the door to one's own heart. It is not an emotional abstract devised to allow hurt, as it is widely understood, but one in which an individual can find all answers so as to restore their heart. It is an important step to initiate the healing process. One could argue that in order to end a relationship, at least one of the partners must make that decision. In physical and real terms this is true. However, to refuse to explore feelings and emotions is in itself a way of running away from a relationship; the relationship with the self. When a relationship ends, it is possible to find numerous excuses and arguments in order to rationalise the situation, and to validate a stance, so as to convince ourselves that it is in fact the ex-lover's own doing what led to this point. This might or might not be true. What is a reality that spreads like a plague through the whole of humanity is that people fear to explore feelings and emotions, what is behind them, so as to find solutions to the emotional reactions that keep taking people to make the same mistakes again and again. There is truth behind the first emotional reaction, a place of inner peace in which anyone can find the solace and comfort that as a norm people try to reach outside of themselves. This kind of truth can be easily recognised due to its emotional resonance, as it has a tremendous impact on the body. In previous pages, the emotional state of heartbreak was given as an example. All one has to do is to resist the reaction. It is the return to love. All doors sought outside are inside. Feeling and emotion is the path that leads there; in the invisible and the intangible. This is what healing is;

how one comes out of the comfort zone and enters the unknown. The term healing can be misleading. It is not that anyone is ill, but that one is disconnected from their own source. As one moves through emotions, new perspectives are created, bringing inner peace.

Shadow work is done and discussed with a partner, but there is an unavoidable step, which is to do it yourself. In a relationship one has the support and love of a partner, making the process more comfortable. There is love, touch, intimacy; a friend that listens and understands. It is in this friend that one finds understanding and compassion. Do not be afraid to accept compassion, nor be put off by the term. Vulnerability makes you stronger as it allows a person to find within the strength and innate abilities that everyone is born with. Not facing this part of the relationship leads to attempts to control a lover in order to recreate a reality that serves selfish needs. It follows the dictate of the inner child in a constant tantrum validating and strengthening the position of ego. In order to find inner strength, one first has to weaken, to surrender to their emotional reality. Claudio Naranjo says, that "in order to become who you are, first you have to experience what you are not". Reality might become ugly, uncomfortable, but once the process is completed, there is a new you waiting, stronger, more real; someone you will recognise through feeling, and at reaching such state, no lover would want to run away. Life becomes possibilities from which both lovers grow. It is a small price to pay for love. Running away from feelings and emotions is a silent lie, an invitation to your lover to end the relationship. The twin flame is interested in growth through love, experience and adventure. The possibilities are there, but if all one does is to seek refuge in self-indulgence as a response to uncomfortable emotions, there will never be, neither growth, nor love. There are other forces within more pleasant and refreshing that the familiar paroxysms of the inner child. First, the reaction must be avoided. Stillness follows opening dimensions into the unknown.

The twin flame might leave the relationship regardless of the work that you do on yourself, as they might not be willing or ready to face this process. Even when one is aware what the process involves or the steps to take, shadow work is not for the faint of heart. In time the runner will have a lot of emotional catch up to do. There is no place to escape from ourselves. If the relationship ended having done your part, be at peace. You are now ready to reunite with the twin flame. This time it could be forever. Let them go; then, see and feel your twin flame coming back.

Being in Love

Being in love is what the term says, a state of being; an enhanced state of consciousness. It embraces the energies required for personal growth and expansion, as well as to create growth in relationships. A person in love displays an extraordinary amount of vital energy. An energy that is always available, within, but to which human beings do not access due to the belief that being in love is only possible when this feeling is projected onto someone else. One can be alone and in love, experiencing the same energy.

Almost everyone who has been in love would have experienced the initial period of euphoria in which everything seems possible. It is followed by a period in which the practicalities of life get in the way. Lovers no longer feel neither the same energy, nor the feeling for the other person nor the passion that is embodied at the beginning. This is due to the excessive focus given to the mundane, a fatal attention that spreads energy in the wrong direction. Without passion or feeling, lovers enter a different stage, where love continues being prevalent, but it is also possible that tense situations arise. It is the period in which partners begin to focus on the flaws and mistakes of their partner. Once the attention is focused on the negative, it is present everywhere to be seen. The lover withdraws to appear only at specific times to meet certain needs. Friendship might have been consolidated, but not necessarily. Initial passion and desire leads people to focus on the physical aspects of the relationship. There will be time to discuss more serious issues. Two lovers could be in a relationship for months without having established the appropriate basis for friendship that helps to support a stronger connection. One may realise that they have been dating a stranger of whom they do not know much about, when a less passionate person wakes up next to them one morning. Being intimate without true intimacy.

It is understandable that during the first weeks or months of the relationship, two people engage in the more passionate expression and physical connection. However, being in love could create endless possibilities by dedicating time and energy to creativity. Love, feeling and passion do not have to pass to a second place after only a few months. It is a reality that could exist in a relationship for the rest of days to come. An obvious disappointment falls upon both partners when the relationship no longer holds the energy and feeling they experienced at the beginning. By this time, they are both wanting to go back to enchanting beginnings, but complaining while watching a film eating pizza. Times of leisure and entertainment are also important, as it is to see if the relationship has become a convenient space to keep the same unhealthy habits of the past, but now with a new lover. One or both partners could feel inclined to blame the other. Thoughts of a new partner and a new relationship that finally makes the permanent spark of love possible may appear. When the relationship solidifies and regresses to a more stagnant and monotonous energy, love might not flow as it used to.

Love in itself is a pure energy that does not require anything else when and if both people could separate the practicalities of life from their emotional output. Unfortunately, humans continue being reactive to challenges, being this work, family relationships or financial issues. Love in the human experience requires constant investment and movement, as well as sacrifices from both partners in order to maintain the flow of the energy in love.

While its energy flows everything seems possible. It create a sense of knowing. It would make sense to follow this energy, but usually the feeling is reserved for the relationship only. It can go and reach farther. The belief that everything is possible feels vibrant and real because it is. Being in love is the perfect timing to make other dreams come true. It is the time to apply for that new job, to engage in creativity, whether it is writing a book, creating a piece of art or to begin a new business. Time to begin an exercise program or to target any other objectives that one may have had in mind. The energy of being in love in unstoppable. There is time for love, intimacy, sex, but every other aspect of life should also be explored. It does not have to end, but for this to happen both people have to invest time and effort that makes it possible. Not only the energy flows, but it expands and grows. It is essential to identify what is important from what is not. Love is an expansive energy that could touch any aspect of life. The interactions with others or the world may differ in nature than that with a lover, but there is no reason for this energy to be limited to a relationship. The purpose is to practice this energy until one becomes accustomed to it, so as to make it permanent. Love is not an energy that happens, it could also be a deliberate act.

Anger is good example that illustrates the previous point. Anger is used to project a powerful energy towards someone or somebody at a particular time. It is an expressive and expansive anger, even though the results oppose to love. Anger is ignited by a trigger to which people react. The actions that follow afterwards varies according to the individual. Someone might explode to let it go immediately, while others might hold it for long periods. The reason anger is so widespread among people and an energy that anyone can connect to easily is due to its constant practice. Anger is perhaps the most practiced energy in the world. It is also a sub-product of fear, but as it is an energy embraced by the majority of the population it is somehow considered normal. It is also proof that humanity lives in fear. Good energies, however, such as love, are relies on the participation of and exchange with others, but it is not an energy that is practiced. This concept is neither ingrained in the human being, nor taught in any school, family home or any other environment. As all things humans, it is an energy that can be trained.

It is also important that both partners dedicate time to their personal activities and interests so as to continue growing. The investment is not merely limited to the relationship, but the self. Creativity in any shape or form energises the flow. It is a wonderful picture to witness your partner returning to you after coming back from an activity that brings renewed joy and energy. This is an exercise that you owe to yourself and to your partner. It is a way of honouring yourself, your partner and life itself. Not only it feels better, it develops a deeper sense of knowing.

Investing in the relationship requires to choose activities carefully. It includes habits and patterns of behaviour. It is as simple as cooking lentils knowing that your girlfriend is deficient in iron, to leave a handwritten, loving note to your boyfriend in the morning or to take the time to find a new place where both of you can visit and have a cup of tea or coffee. It is the thought, the improvisation, the walk to that new coffee shop, whether is sunny or raining. It is the act of opening the door to your partner whether you are male or female, to act in reverence as you do, the playfulness; the complicit smile. Love is movement that can become a perfect choreography, yet be spontaneous. Love is in the simple things. To stop seeking these activities in a relationship should be a warning sign that it might not be going in the right direction. Modern society as it is established reunites all the elements and facilities for the human being to become sedentary. Once a relationship is formally settled, it is as important to choose energising activities and goals as it is to avoid those that instead of creating a positive energy subtracts it instead. To give an example, when an individual feels happy and in a good state of mind, there is a certain proclivity to celebrate. Many of these celebrations are neither healthy, nor bring anything positive.

Often celebrations in modern society include consuming alcohol and/or food that may seem a good idea on that one evening, but which carries damaging consequences the next morning. More often than not, such celebrations are overindulgent. Drinking or eating excessively are the most frequent. In the age of information there is no longer excuse to see alcohol as a social glue. Such permissive attitude towards such a toxic substance only serves to continue the prevalence of ignorance. Humanity needs to find alternatives to socialising and interacting with others. These alternatives already exist. Being selective with the activities one takes on, may exclude others that up to the present moment have been part of the daily routine. When done sporadically one does not have to be alarmed about the consequences of overindulging every now and then. When celebrations of this type occur too often, the person's energy withers leading to seek more temporary comfort, but now seeing it as a distraction from the real issue, being this, that one has disconnected from their original source of energy. What one has to look for is when the intake, which is not limited to edibles or liquids-causes to damage a person's body, mind or the integrity of their wellbeing. Modern consumerism is overloaded with traps and temptations that only serve to keep a person sedentary, as well as creating a feeling that one constantly needs more of it. Instant gratification comes under many different wraps. To get to yes, one might have to say no often.

The same principle applies to the company we keep or the places that one visits. Not everyone around you has their best interest in your wellbeing. Some of the people that surround you may just be lurking, waiting to see what they can get or to extract some of that vital and empowering energy. Being in love is a magnet to all sorts of people. Often when people fall in love and begin a relationship perceive the interest of other suitors. They might have gone through a long period in which no one showed any interest, despite their effort and the will to meet someone special. When being single extends to long periods of time, the idea of someone special may be removed, at which point people do settle for someone not that special, after the belief that someone is better than no one at all. Being in a relationship, whether there person that one has settle for is that special one or the alternative not so special creates a shining energy around the subject. There is a high degree of arrogance in accepting the advances of others during a relationship when functioning on this energy, and which at times leads to people being unfaithful. It is taking the gift of love for granted, as well as spreading an energy thin. Practising love also come with responsibility. When lust or vanity are mixed in order to satisfy immediate desires, one remains into the known, as these actions are selfish and non-expansive.

Imagine instead, your partner returning to you beaming after they have been carried out an activity that makes them feel vibrant, energised and full of vital energy. They cannot wait share the experience with you, to tell how complete and energised they feel. It is a spectacle of true beauty and love that they want to share with you. While this may have been an activity that serves to improve them personally, the energy is redirected to the relationship. Listen to what they have to say, with the intimacy of silence allowing yourself to feel the energy flowing and filling the space. At reaching this level of personal satisfaction, what your partner will seek from then on is more of such activities, to recreate the same feeling and energy once again. When people experience such amounts of happiness due to their investment in their personal development, they are also happy with what they have, in this case having and immediate and healthy effect on a relationship that is being fuelled by loving energy. It is self-loved redirected towards a partner and the relationship. With both lovers committed to their personal development, the relationship grows in strength and intimacy. It is essential to give time and space to a partner, especially when they are involved in activities that contribute to their personal growth. It is equally important that you do find time and space for the same purpose.

If one is not aware of the possibilities for growth within a relationship, it is never too late to begin. These activities can be taken on at any time. Even a onetime activity that injects such vibrant energy makes an overwhelming difference to the relationship. One has to expand the concept of creativity to every daily activity. Creativity is not reduced merely to the arts. Making a sandwich is creativity, as it is to start or expand a business or producing a plan that explores new possibilities within the relationship. Use your imagination and work with what you have. It does not have to be a costly enterprise. More costly is to be involved in an unfulfilled relationship or to live a loveless life.

Single people can follow the same steps, as a couple would do in order to increase their energy levels and optimism for life. Waiting for a lover to appear so as to begin to enjoy life is a betrayal to the self. While single, one can use this period to improve the relationship with the self. As personal growth takes place, the energy creates a magnetic field that attracts what they seek. It is more likely to attract people with whom one can fall in love when energy levels are high. Whether you are single or in a relationship, take steps to fall in love. The energy is within. Love is a verb that requires movement, a healthy input and engagement in energising and loving activities. Make peace with the current situation. Accept it. Get curious. Keep moving. Be creative. This is all it takes.

Manifesting the Twin Flame

The term twin flame is closely associated with spirituality. One of the problems derived of the general understanding of spirituality is that at times it gets lost in translation. Spirituality is everyone and everything. The tangible and the intangible. The visible and the invisible. Spirituality is also associated with a number of set practices. However, spiritual practices do not make anyone more spiritual than others. These practices help people in their spiritual growth, as it induces specific states of being, as well as improving someone's discipline and self-control. It is up to each individual what practices they choose and how to use them. Other people obtain the similar results in their personal development through different activities and ways of life. The spirit is always within. Everyone is free to express it as they wish. Someone could learn the same or similar principles by reading a type of books that might not specifically treat spiritual matters, yet, both, love and the soul can be found anywhere. Others might develop such knowledge and practices naturally, perhaps following intuition. A family's education often serves the same purpose. Regardless of what practices are followed or what one may learn by reading a book, attending retreats or seminars, it is essential to apply these principles to daily life. Knowing the principle alone is not enough.

In regards to the twin flame, there is a variety of information that contributes to make this figure a mythological one. This point has been discussed in the chapter 'Debunking the Myth.' Throughout this book the reader might have already perceived some clues as to why someone might meet with their twin flame, as well as why they might not. Leading a spiritual life may or may not make the twin flame a reality. Spirituality requires action, to apply principles, practices and beliefs to our way of life. An example of how someone may be implementing this is meditation. Some people dedicate a fixed amount of time to this practice, while others might be able to connect to a meditative state throughout the day while going on about their routine. One way of understanding or applying is no better or worse than the other, just different. It is every individual's choice how they choose to apply it in their experience. There is not the right way or the wrong way. Everyone must choose what they deem appropriate for their personal growth.

There are no guarantees that you will meet the twin flame, no matter what literature or others may say. Fully understanding the concept and the purpose of such encounter might discourage many people from wanting to manifest such experience, as it is a destructive process of the self that some might not be prepared or willing to go through.

"What you are seeking is seeking you," says Osho. You will meet your twin flame once you are ready, not before. He also says; "what you are seeking, you already are." Waiting for someone to appear in our life to rescue us from ourselves or the life we have been leading is not the answer. This way of understanding life or love is no different from waiting for father or mother to come back home and lighten up the day. It requires a more proactive approach. Meeting the twin flame brings us to the beautiful, deep and meaningful reality of discovering ourselves, thus, seeking the twin flame is an effort worth to encourage. As mentioned in a previous chapter, the twin flame is likely to be leading a life in which they are seeking the best part of themselves. This process requires great effort, discipline, energy and integrity. In order to do so, it is possible that a person leads a solitary life, detached from relationships that no longer serve them. The intention in this case is to create a nurturing space for new relationships that facilitates growth. Integrity allows to recognise and then decide whether the possibilities that are presented are what is needed or what is wanted. There is a substantial difference between both. It is as important to discard what it is obviously negative, as it is to renounce to an attractive experience that could cause a distraction from the real aim. A solitary life when permanent is not the answer. Seeking the higher self is a sacred experience. Sacredness has to be understood as s person being the sacred vessel that sails through all possibilities within for personal expansion, considering at all times how these choices may affect who they are. It does not have to carry religious connotations. What is accepted in our current reality determines what comes next. The elements mentioned in this paragraph provide solidity and strength in an individual to continue seeking what they truly want. Follow the feeling. In the way to it, there will be an abundance of distractions and false truths hidden behind illusory veils. It is possible that one continues projecting self-delusions on people they meet and future experiences, in order to recreate the image that the mind has created of what love and life must look like. There is also the possibility that others try to sell the perfect expression of love. There is love, truth, integrity and authenticity in everyone. Love is the expression you give it. In the same way that someone is capable to recognise their emotional truth by applying principles and beliefs to their experience, they will be able to recognise it in others. Removing the importance of what others do, say or may offer is often essential to maintain integrity. It is a process of complete dedication to self-expression and self-knowledge. Whom to share this experience with is a personal choice. Being selective is not the same as excluding others systematically. Once the experience is shared there will be those who agree, as well as those who disagree. The selection is natural.

The priority in this process is to choose yourself. Every action taken is to honour yourself. The attention has to be focused on the self, directing all energy to personal development. Personal development does not have to be a process with allocated times. The flexibility in the process allows to apply it to every part of life. It can be applied to work, domestic tasks, relationships with others and any daily activity. It could be a lifetime dedication. It is a matter of adding these practices, values and energy to the daily routine. The steps taken are intended to define you as a better person by removing old habits, beliefs and patterns of behaviour that halt possibilities for you to become whole again. Choosing yourself does not equal to being selfish. Removing beliefs includes the illusion that one can only be happy or in love while in a relationship. One can be happy and single. Being single for a period of time allows anyone enough time and space to increment the amount of activities that serve you. Time alone has to be understood as an opportunity, not a reason to dwell on your current marital status. As the feeling of wellbeing increases, once a lover appears it is easier to attract their interest, as well as keeping them interested. However, this process of transformation is not intended to attract a lover. The lover will come attracted by energy. It is a time for self-improvement. The previous chapter 'Being in love' encourages acts of self-love and activities that support personal expansion and growth. To know what activities to choose one can look at personal interests, hobbies or projects. The list varies according to the individual, but there is not a specific activity that one must choose. It is the freedom to choose that makes it inviting.

The attitude to take on this new challenge is close to obsessive. Only with this determination one can achieve results. If you are reading this book, it is possible that you have grown tired on the old ways leading to the same places. The satisfaction of past days when engaging in such activities is no longer there. You do want more, but do not know where to turn to. You are in the right place.

There is no magic wand that will bring a twin flame nor any other lover. The physical twin flame appears when one is seeking themselves. Single people continually hope to meet a match. One keeps their eyes and senses open to the multiple possibilities social life offers. But it is not the priority. The twin flame is a seeker of truth. The progression is painful, as new experiences reveal parts of the self that one avoided thus far. It is a reason for celebration. One has to remember that in every process of transformation having fun is also a powerful tool to achieve results. It does not have be a path of pain and suffering, but fun and joy. The belief that all transformation is painful and full of suffering is a sub-product of Christian mythology. Fun makes this adventure a source of energy. This is also shadow work. Anyone can do it alone. In this case without the reflection or feedback of a romantic lover. The key is the degree of involvement and passion invested. Even though one is single and may feel lonely, life offers numerous mirrors on a daily basis. Shadow work can be undertaken in a professional position, with friends, family and everyone else that crosses our paths. Everyone has a glimpse of the twin flame in their eyes and hearts at a closer look.

The moment the focus is turned to the self, one becomes the observer and the subject. Both are the same person, watching their own actions, character and behaviour. Being the observer one can detach from their own experience and have a laugh at themselves with love and compassion. It is laughing at the serious dedication that it is employed in being adults. We are nothing but children in adult bodies doing our best to interpret what an adult is supposed to be and act like it. A mystery no one has yet managed to decipher. Everyone is aware of their own limitations or what they believe to be limitations. Most of them are self-imposed. It is time to ask questions, to seek answers. In order to help the process, one can take stock of their life and open the drawer of unfinished projects. Everyone has one filled with dust, webs and forgotten dreams. The steps to be taken do not have to be epic. Simple steps suffice. For some people writing a simple poem would uplift their energy, while for others, clearing the space that surrounds them would create a similar effect. It might be the time to do attend the gym that one has been paying for, but not visiting regularly. The options are limitless. And so are you. Limitless. Most of the projects people never carry out are due to simple reasons. Someone might be waiting for circumstances to change and improve. Others might believe that it would be much easier to take on new ventures once they had secured everything on their long list of priorities: to meet a new partner, to have the ideal body, to have more money. The excuses to procrastinate and indulge in apathy are endless. These are all excuses not to meet the real self by exploring personal gifts and talents. The guitar that is gathering dust in the closet has to be rescued and used as a tool to meet the best version of you.

Being single does not mean that one has to go through the entire process alone. Let's put everything into perspective and look at the alternatives. Seeking new challenges opens new paths. Nothing better than meeting new people. There are support groups, meet up groups and numerous organised social gatherings that provide an incredible network and resources for personal development. It is not imperative to do this alone. Humans are social creatures. According to character and beliefs, some people may decide to take a more spiritual approach such as retreats or group meditations or alternatives avenues that provide space for growth. Someone else might choose to build a shed in their garden an invite others to participate,

Coming out of the comfort zone is another element to keep in mind if one wants to achieve best results. The comfort zone is the familiar space in which one feels comfortably safe, but never entirely happy. More than a comfortable zone one could look at it as a prison area in which everyone finds a minimum levels of contentment. There is nothing to lose. The purpose of engaging in a journey of self-discovery is to remove learned behaviour that has become part of someone's identity, but at the same time prevents a person from becoming whole by exploring their gifts and passions. Do what makes you happy and what you fear most. Whether this is public speaking, a yoga class or sending a novel to a publisher which was never sent due to fear of rejection, it is time to take steps that bring the best in you. Fear of rejection turns into acceptance of rejection through building enough strength to understand it and live with it. One can always try again, and again, and again. This is also shadow work, to immerse in feelings and emotions, which have been avoided due to fear.

As an incentive, the twin flame is likely to be in the same process of self-development, seeking and exploring the missing parts of the self. One of the twin flames might be more committed to the process than the other. If you are reading this book, do not count on the possibility that they are reading it too. They are probably leading a more organic and dedicated life, writing their own book through experience. The twin flame probably has a clearer understanding that it is a process that has to be done alone, reason for which in the eventuality that both meet, they might be reticent to accommodate anyone's needs or hear what they have to offer. Perhaps it is not the right time and never will be. Knowing what one needs at the time does not have to be confused with what one wants. One has to realise that one of the key elements is that proactive seeking makes the energy attractive to the other, which is not the same as being looking for a twin flame. Seeking for the self comes first. There is a substantial difference in both views that need to be differentiated. One of the twin flames might be more advanced than the other in the process with a wider and deeper understanding of the issues they face, or the steps to be taken. In the event of meeting it would not make a significant difference, as they are ever supportive of the other. However, they will resist any input that may deter their progress. They will be clear about this point. This factor may have a major impact on deciding whether to start a relationship or not. A relationship is not a priority. Wholeness is, and so it is inner peace.

The importance of overcoming fears by following your heart, engaging in activities to make you come to life and help and support you in becoming the best version of yourself cannot be emphasised enough at this point. When seeking, everything that is needed appears; people, places, insights or anything else that is required. Seeking with the heart magnetises both, needs and desires. The twin flame wants to see and experience your authenticity. If at any point indecisions, fears or doubts take over, the twin flame will see it as another period of stagnation incompatible with their process. This can only bring further tension, but also opportunities for growth. Pause is always a healthy choice. For one of the twin flames, a romantic liaison might to be as important as it is to the other, and definitely not an essential component. They can live without it or so they think. The twin flame will separate in order to preserve the value and rewards of the hard work they put into growth even if they must say farewell when they are in love. There is no truth in what reasons anyone may have to believe they can do better alone, unless the relationship is unhealthy or abusive. They are both committed to themselves and uncompromising with others. Priorities could differ. Someone may see the relationship as a space for growth, while the other may feel that it requires too much energy. The more creative energy that is added, as well as to personal growth the more the energy flows. The probabilities that the relationship ends are high. The twin flame is probably by now someone with a greater purpose, following intuition's strong call and inner wisdom, being on a mission that transforms life, in which detachment and prioritising themselves play become essential instruments in becoming who they truly are. Some people believe that relationships interfere with their personal development. The only person who can stop such growth is ourselves. The reality they are seeking is a space, a feeling of wellbeing and inner peace. When the physical reality does not match the space they are in or they are seeking, if they have enough experience and awareness they will not be afraid to continue the journey alone.

Spiritual practices at this stage can help, but not necessarily. Meditation aids in gaining a sense of inner peace and wholeness when practiced regularly. Do as much exercise as possible to maintain high levels of energy. The intensity of emotions deplete the body of vital energy misleading the mind to depressive thinking. The less energy, the more movement that is required. Yoga is a wonderful vehicle to gain strength and relaxation. Through deliberate movement it is possible to reconnect with the body, connecting to their personal and physical space. It improves posture, flexibility and breathing. Breathing exercises are also a great source of support to regain a higher state of consciousness, as well as providing immediate release of energy and bringing a sense of inner peace. By only paying conscious attention to breathing, states of being are altered. The importance of movement during a period of intense emotions is vital to maintain a composed perspective during the relationship. A relationship might not survive without it.

Spiritual practices could also disrupt the process. It is important not to get lost in rituals. Differentiate between practices and pose. Often the time used in the preparation of rituals could be dedicated to more meaningful practices. Candles, incense and mantras might play a part in such practices, but they are not essential. Feeling speaks volumes about the practices one follows. Often the engagement in spiritual practices lacks the depth and determination that shadow work requires. Keep it simple.

In order to improve confidence or low self-esteem get involved in the creative process. Seek activities to perform alone, with your partner and others. The chapter 'Being in love' offers some guidance and ideas, leaving plenty of room and freedom for each seeker to use their imagination. If you do not believe that you have imagination or a creative mind, begin with imagining what you would do with your life if money was never an issue, and get excited about it. Everyone has an imagination. To use it or not is a choice. There is no step by step guidance to what one must or must not do in order to reunite with the twin flame. These are abstracts open to interpretation, personal perspective and experience. It is an energy we create and follow. Authenticity, love, integrity, creativity, kindness, vulnerability or compassion are portals to new realities that one must enter and experience through feeling. Results might not be achieved the first day, but with persistence and commitment states of being do change, bringing a sense of accomplishment and wellbeing. It does not have to be a slow process.

In spite of the personal input, effort and the energy invested in the relationship, your partner might still run away for reasons only known to them or might not even be willing to start it. In a sense, the journey of self-discovery is a selfish path. Selfish in the sense that they need time and space to achieve what they want without taking anything from anyone. At the same time, they cannot afford to have anything taken from them. It preserves their intention, health and energy. Any kind of personal relationship or attachment that might stop them from growing, especially if one of the partners cannot follow their pace, is a space they will not enter if they feel that something is being taken from them. The separation is heart breaking. It is possible that it does not make any sense, nor has a logical explanation. The runner chooses themselves in order to grow for multiple reasons. The possibilities of the unknown and the thirst for a creative life cancels reason and logic. There is an inner vision, a feeling that must be followed and fulfilled that is met in the unknown, where reason might not be the best guide to follow. Once a person reaches certain depth in their self-development, the way they make choices varies from the logical methods of the past. The inner call is more powerful that safety or any offering of everlasting love. Not every person needs a relationship in order to be happy. The priority is self-love, which does oppose romantic relationships, but this could be the way in which is understood. Every day the twin flame stands on a fence. There are possibilities, but no certainty. Keeping yourself interested, energised and creative serves to keep a partner interested. Seek neither certainty, nor safety. Every day is a new adventure. Adventures are full of surprises. How one responds to them determines what happen next. If the intention of one of the partners is certainty, this could be understood as an attempt to coerce freedom. A successful relationship is dynamic, one does not write words on a stone.

There must be a natural evolution. Of course, reaching a common ground, so as to define the nature, as well as the possibilities that a couple encounter is theme for intimate discussions. These agreements, when flexible, can be modified and developed as the relationship advances. The journey of self-discovery is one of freedom. Anything that threatens this energy will be interpreted as such. The runner does not need many reasons to leave. Let's not give them any.

Modern society encourages individuality, but neither authenticity nor originality. There is a prerequisite of uniformity in order to belong and to be accepted. In the quest for authenticity avoiding comparison with others offers another transformative tool in which one can confidently articulate a true voice. Comparing yourself to others leads to constant disappointment. One of the driving, but also damaging forces in modern society is competition. Every individual is unique. No one can do what others do in the same unique way. The futility in trying to emulate others or their achievements ends in frustration and disappointment, a feeling that one is not good enough. Practising and developing our own talents help to remove this belief. Mimicking others one remains within the limiting confinements of a false belief trying to reach out for the impossible. In this case what and how others achieve. What others will admire about you, if immediate validation is what is needed, is authenticity, one's own uncompromising, colourful expression. It is time that the world realises that individuality is something to praise, to be encouraged, not only by others, but by the self. This is achieved by acquiring self-confidence. Developing talents and gifts increase confidence. Anyone has the ability to surprise themselves when committing to exploring their natural gifts to what they have so far believed are limitations. A writer that does not write will never fully understand their talent, but neither the athlete that does not challenge themselves in training.

It is not time to conform, nor to seek validation. Facing insecurities is another phase of shadow work. The steps are repeated again and again in different situations. The process is endless, with the understanding that nothing is neither solid, nor permanent. Everything changes, everything is in constant movement. If life becomes overwhelming at times it is only due to the human being's inability to keep moving, to accept change or evolve with the times. Keep moving. Ideology and beliefs do play against this process, as they become absolutes in the human psyche. Beliefs are created in the mind, but they do take over the body energetically. When a belief is challenged and cannot find a healthy response, an uncomfortable emotion arises, followed by a consequent emotional reaction. Once the concept of shadow work is understood it becomes easier to experience the numerous challenges. At the same time, one may gain wisdom by understanding a challenge as an opportunity, a portal to new knowledge. Beliefs do change throughout life with age and experience. Self-development and/or a relationship, not necessarily with the twin flame, accelerates these processes. Movement is internal, as well as external. There is a natural reaction to challenging elements in each individual, for which reason it becomes essential to learn to create a healthy response that can be found in pause and reflection. In a previous chapter, silence was suggested as a tool to allow intimacy in conversations with a lover. When facing challenges to beliefs that have become absolutes, silence is equally beneficial in order to learn from the situation. In the relationship with the self, the conversation is internal. Watch how you talk to yourself, and while listening learn to distinguish if what you hear are the words and ideas of others, or your own. It is equally important to challenge ourselves, to stop the endless, self-defeating rhetoric that we are not enough by allowing silence to take over internal conversation. Silent as a response provides a bottomless well of wisdom. It is more confusing and exhausting to try and defend a firm belief, as it requires explanations that rationalise why someone believes what they believe, than to examine a new idea or belief remaining reactionless. Against popular belief, silence does not mean acquiescence. There is wisdom in silence. It is no different from a child attending school. Children do listen in order to learn the lesson from a teacher. Every situation is a lesson. An immediate response indicates that one is not open to learn, as well as a degree of arrogance and intolerance towards new concepts, implying that we know it all. Of course, not all stimuli is filled with wisdom, as not everyone is a qualified or wise teacher. Often the speaker's best speech could be silence instead. Collective consciousness is crammed with false beliefs that continues being broadcasted from mouth to mouth, in order to prove what we know or we do not, often imposing our own views by enforcing the projection of the self over others. It only contributes to add more emotional debris to the noise of the world. In this process there is no need to disprove others, but to develop the most authentic version of the self, embodying a character that moves through obstacles unmoved by the false rhetoric of the world. The world is what it is. One responds with silence, without reaction, using their energy to achieve what they want instead. In correcting others, even in thought, one loses a great part of life. It creates unwanted thoughts that continue circling in the mind without purpose.

So much movement could lead to an emotional storm with the consequent reactions. It could be either internalised or externalised. The first reaction could cause depression. Again, movement and creativity help to deal with this experience. An external reaction may lead to disagreement, seeking validation or comfort from a partner, which may translate into arguments or separation. It is essential to find time and space to be alone in order to process new information about the world, ideas or personal impressions. Yoga helps to calm down, bring inner peace and balance, as it provides both movement and stillness. Meditation helps to empty the mind. A simple walk alone could be enough for this purpose. The aim is to find comfortable spaces in which to recharge energy. It is as important to allow yourself to do nothing, as it is to move. In every situation and experience balance delivers a healthy outcome. In the process one learns that nothing is under control and that the healthy response is adaptability and flexibility in every situation. This is a journey within, therefore there could be an overwhelming amount of inner, emotional movement, which is the part that one can control; the response to stimuli. Mistakes would be made.

When understood as lessons that help to bring balance to the inner self, these mistakes will not be repeated. Once again a reminder to have a laugh, to engage in fun activities, focusing on love. There is strong resistance in the human being to dedicate efforts and energy to self-love, what leads to seek the love of another. What matters is that we love. To love another, is in many ways to love the self. What we do to others, we do to ourselves. Love in any expression is the best classroom for self-discovery, although it should not be constantly focused outwards or directed towards a lover. An act of self-love can be as simple as dedicating time and space to find solace, such as meditation or any form of physical exercise. Physical exercise is in itself creative, as time, efforts and energy are dedicated to improve the body, what eventually has a positive and healthy influence in the mind. Every interaction with the world, including those with a lover, is an opportunity to learn. It is a matter of shaping perspective in order to see that within every situation, there is a possibility, that every problem contains the answer. Movement creates the necessary spontaneity required to advance in the adventure of the self, while stillness allows self-reflection. Modern society promotes passivity. Humanity's lack of spontaneity only serves to suffocate the most creative and authentic part of the self, translating into the current portrait of uniformity that clouds the world.

Every healthy, creative step you take towards meeting and reaching out towards yourself is a step towards the twin flame. Get up and get out there. Everything is a paradox.

When there is a positive movement towards the external world, there is also movement in the inner world.

Transcending the Twin Flame

In the worst case scenario, the relationship has now ended. Heartbreak fills the space that at the same time feels empty. However painful the experience is, perspective is a must at this stage, but so it is compassion. Compassion and self-compassion should always be present in someone's life, as its energy embraces an individual in a space of warmth and understanding. We try too hard, too often to keep achieving making strenuous efforts for long periods of time, not allowing enough resting time. The period preceding the separation from a relationship can be as stressful, as it is draining, using and projecting all energy to contain or trying to improve the situation. Separating from a lover is a devastating experience that renders people to an unrecognisable state, a shadow of the self. Compassion offers the silence and calmness that somehow contains a person's energy in order to deal with their feelings and emotions. Both states, depression and heartbreak

Heartbreak is a coin with two different faces. One being the devastating feeling of longing and pain for the loss of a lover. The other is rebirth. Understanding heartbreak as a rebirth one can begin to take healthy steps towards recovery. The forms of the quest might have changed, but the purpose remains. Heartbreak is a place of surrender. It is a space that differs from depression, and even though both have similitudes there are differences between one and the other.

It is human tendency to over indulge in heartbreak, quite understandably, as it is an excruciating and traumatic experience. There is never a right time for heartbreak. It is necessary to point out the similitude with the moment of birth, when a child leaves the comfort and protective space in their mother's womb to be introduced to a fairly hostile environment in which he or she begins to form a sense of independence, however supporting or loving the new surroundings may be. Heartbreak could be experienced at different times during childhood. How it occurs varies according to each individual, their personal experience and interpretation of events. It is never the same for everyone. Not every child that is born enters the world voluntarily. Some children offer more resistance than others. The moment of birth can be traumatic and heart breaking. The first encounters mentioned in previous chapters with fear in which a child must decide to accept and conform to the standard and imposed ways that causes separation from inner wisdom in order to find acceptance and a sense of belonging are heart breaking experiences that one might have blocked deep in their subconscious or simply cannot remember. The energetic impact of the experience remains in the body. Energetic experiences stored in the subconscious contribute to the creation of the inner child and the desire to control life from that moment on, for which people create an array of irrational resources that serve to manipulate their environment.

It is time to let go or at least to create the intention. Let go of beliefs, the will to control and the attachment to the lost lover. During a period of surrender after the break-up, everything loses meaning. Plans were made for two people, but now one finds themselves in a position in which they are alone. It is the perfect opportunity to silence old beliefs, to begin a new life after a period of rest and self-reflection. Letting go is an exercise intended to choose yourself as suggested all along in this text. One of the difficulties in understanding the progression of letting go is that as one tries and learns to let go of another, energy, feelings, emotions and thoughts continue being focused on someone else.

The emotional impact on a person drastically depletes their vital energy. They function on survival mode. The mind has a proclivity towards negative thinking and self-defeatism maintaining low levels of energy. It is also time to surrender, to accept what is. It is not the end, but the beginning. Understanding heartbreak as a rebirth allows to take baby steps setting all the pieces together once again in different positions and order. Now you are your own father and mother. This is another wonderful possibility: to become the parent you always wanted to have. The process of self-discovery has not changed. The difference is that one continues life alone. Throughout this journey an individual has accumulated enough knowledge and experience to deal with this phase in life that allows to gain perspective, understanding and overcoming it successfully. The ability of any human being for transformation and personal evolution is one of the most underestimated. Heartbreak has the advantage that as vital energy drops to its lowest levels, one has no option but to preserve it, using it for their own benefit. Energy is contained. It is time to be unapologetic in not offering this essential energy to others. It contributes to create healthy boundaries, setting a memory for future interactions that either allow or discard external elements into someone's personal space. The privacy, the need for personal space and solitude naturally created after heartbreak provides an ideal scenario to become the observer, setting strong intentions for what is yet to come. One does not want to return to the old ways, but to create new paths. There will be time to contribute with energy to the wellbeing of the world and others in ways that do not drain their energy. Heartbreak is also the space where the creative process begins. Every step suggested leads to the same place; the most authentic self. Heartbreak may seem a step back in the process, but if this is what you are currently experiencing or it is a past experience, it is and was necessary. As it is given, never chosen, it is natural to reject it, what it might delay the moment of surrender to what is.

During these setbacks people do not have a choice but to stop to rest, reflect, and in time, consider future options. To see alternative ways of living and the possibilities ahead. Choosing wellbeing, authenticity and integrity, the energy initially focused to bring an ex-lover back is redirected inwards. The minimum energy someone is left with hardly allows them to cover the bare necessities. This energy that does not have the magnetism. Trying to use it to bring a lover back is a futile exercise.

Along with the baby steps taken to rebuild a strong sense of self, common sense suggests to use this period as a time to rest, take good care of yourself and self-reflection. There are numerous ways in which to nurture yourself, such as resting, a healthy diet, choosing simple and pleasant activities that one has wanted to experience, but neglected to carry out, keeping hydrated, a short break in a different location, keeping good and healthy company. Each of these choices can become a guide to self-love. It is also time to put every transformational tool that one has acquired during the process to good use. Listen to yourself. Your true self is a compassionate being. Compassion begins with the self. The feeling of rejection could transform into a process of self-rejection. Someone might feel underserving of the best things in life, which might not be different from the life someone has experienced that far. Often a relationship serves to break with the monotony and hardships of an existence of lack, which in a large number of people is self-induced due to an unconscious belief. Compassion is a must.

Listening and silence are now powerful vehicles to create a brighter reality than the one previously known. The purpose is to create a new vision in which a person can thrive by reconnecting all parts of their being. Be compassionate and understanding. Removing negativity from self-talk can be done by silencing the voice within. One of the traces that heartbreak leaves is the feeling that one is not enough, what in turn leads to repeatedly questioning a large void that do not have any answers. Silence is the answer. Questions that do not have answers indicate lack of acceptance causing further anxiety, loneliness and a feeling of not being understood. However pleasant being understood is, we do not need to be understood when we understand ourselves. Most of the questions asked during this period do not have logical answers. It is also a misuse of the imagination, as well as exhausting, requiring an excessive amount of energy to think. You may master the limitless power of the imagination or become a slave to it. Both options are trained thought. There is hope, a much better future to be created when someone finds the determination to continue the journey of self-discovery. The feeling of heartbreak in a person intensifies after the relationship, particularly in people with a sense of incompleteness before it began. A reminder that being single and alone offers an opportunity to reconcile with the relationship and friendship that an individual has with themselves. It is OK not to feel OK.

Heartbreak does not last forever. However painful the experience may be or how hard someone has been hit by it, eventually the energy returns to body and mind. Trying to rush the process will not help. This part of the process may seem slower. Slowness has to be understood as a training ground in which one learns deliberate movements that can be performed at a faster pace once energy is restored. Nothing lasts forever. Everything is temporary. This is also human condition.

Taking heartbreak as the ideal space for transformation, one can begin to familiarise with the qualities and energy of the creative process. First, there is wide and general misunderstanding of what creative energy is due to stereotypes and comparison with the great masters, as well as what the concept of art is or should be. While it is necessary to define everything we come in contact with, in order to understand it, or how to apply it in practical terms, absolute definitions solidify the essence of art and creative energy, the opposite of its true nature. What solidifies dies, as it stands against the constant movement of life. Both art and creative energy are ever expanding. It cannot be confined to a strict definition. Such perception limits its many purposes and uses. Both creative energy and imagination are endless. How imagination is used so as to hit time and again imposed limitations that prevent the expansion of consciousness and the evolution of humanity, is up to every individual. From this perspective, the mind is commonly inclined to create limiting and loveless scenarios that restrain any kind of progression. This trained thought is the result of adapting to a system which does not encourage expansive learning through feeling, emotion and creativity in the child, in order to find acceptance and a sense of belonging. Picasso or Michelangelo were great artists, and they are recognised as such. Comparison with the great masters makes art intimidating, as well as misleading.

Creative energy is inherent to the human being. It is a bottomless source of abundance and vital energy, mostly misused, if not completely ignored. Engaging in a creative process is a magical way out of the depressive mechanisms of heartbreak. It is not necessary to create a masterpiece to exhibit in the most acclaimed galleries in the world, nor to gain a name as an artist. It is a process in which someone makes their life a masterpiece. This is all it takes. At this stage, finding the energy to create or even to be able to focus on creativity might prove to be a hard exercise. Imagination is a creative tool that can be trained by visualising the desired outcome to introduce positive and healthy energy. Seeing a goal materialised increases the levels of vital energy. Allow yourself a slow start without prior impositions leaving space for spontaneity, improvisation and the ability to surprise yourself. Creativity is flexible. There are no rules to be followed. It might not be possible to sit eight hours to write a novel, so let's begin with twenty minutes or an hour. A novel is a good example. However, one does not have to involve themselves in any creative process that involves art per se. Art is an amazing tool for growth, but not everyone has the inner call to produce such work. The example of a novel is ideal in this case, as at the beginning what one finds is a blank page that now has to be filled with words and ideas. Inspiration might prove to be evasive too. The secret of inspiration is to do the work, to dedicate time to create. Inspiration comes when one is looking for it, not the other way around. This is another misconception, based on the general myth that when inspiration comes, the poet writes the poem. Nothing further from the truth. The poet seeks inspiration first, then finds it. As the poet has established a healthy, permanent connection with creative energy more thoughts, ideas an inspiration may appear, but a proactive engagement in the creative process is necessary. The poet has to write the first word, then a verse and so on.

Creative energy can be used to make a table, redecorate the house or to make a plan to create a home business. There are no limits. Making a sandwich or cooking a more elaborate dish is creativity. The essence of this energy is found in the internal movement. Access to it might not be easy at first, which it could be disappointing. Keep going. This is why it is also important to find discipline to continue with the project. For this reason it is advisable not to set specific goals trying to write for eight hours every day, as it might not be possible. Such approach could be overwhelming and exhausting, creating an illusion of limitation, feelings of not being good enough. While it is important to set a strong intention and a defined goal, such as writing a book, every step in the process must allow for flexibility to change direction at any time. To pause and rest is a healthy step. Procrastination is not. Procrastination is fear; fear of knowing who you really are. The first step is always a blank canvas. Everything else has to be added.

Whether the process involves writing a book, starting a business or baking a cake, all these activities require the first step, followed by many others.

Creative energy is easily recognisable through feeling when one is connected to it. It is an energy that takes on a life of its own. It is so magnetic, so exuberant and uncontainable that as one goes along, they will find more time and space to create. These moments become a date with yourself. While dating yourself, the observer will perceive environment and the energy that makes it a transformative experience. Consequently, another memory is created, which the body automatically stores, becoming an invaluable point of reference for future dates and experiences that will allow to recognise which energy is acceptable and which one is not. If it does not feel right, it is probably not right. Every situation, every moment is an opportunity to explore new possibilities. Such is the process of creation; endless. One does not have to take on every project or to accomplish each goal that comes to mind. What remains is the knowing that the possibilities are there; to realise that there are different options. Training yourself to recognise this information is part of the creative process. Eventually the process becomes a series of encounters with the self, a source of energy and dynamism. This part of the process is about becoming excited. It does take practice and determination from the beginning. Whatever one produces, if it is not satisfactory, it can be discarded to begin again. Start with small project and remove judgment. If the creation is not as satisfactory as one would wish, a small project allows to begin again or to do it in a different way. The creation in itself is not important, connecting to creative energy is, and this takes practice. There will be time in the future to perfect the process. What begins small now might become a source of income or a creative space for cooperation with others with a more focused intention, such a business or a meeting place that creates community for other people with similar goals.

The other quality of creative energy is that it becomes a part of the self, a practice that turns into a habit. The purpose is to produce a different kind of energy that might have not been used since childhood. This energy is vibrant. As energy grows within, it manifests physically. Eventually this energy takes over, so it can be used in everything and everywhere. It is a certain way to fall in love again, with life, with the self, as well as creating a magnetic field to attract what is desired. While reuniting with this energy might not happen immediately, it is certain to appear.

The important elements in the creative energy and the creative process are the feelings, the emotions and the inner resourcefulness that one meets along the way. It is the reconnection to one's true essence. In this state of being is to let go occurs naturally. Heartbreak becomes an experience of the past, and while feelings for a lost lover might still be in mind and heart, their presence is no longer the product of desperate necessity or the overwhelming sense of loneliness. Heartbreak, like every other experience in life is relative, according to the importance that it is given to it at the time. In this case, one can see it as a trigger to rediscover the self or to engage in a more positive life; a point of inflection. Maybe heartbreak is the result of having led an unfulfilling life that collapses in order to provoke a change in attitude and general outlook. Human beings have the natural ability to alchemise any state of being, any situation if allowed. The loss of connection with our inner resources make of alchemy a romantic term that only exists in books and fantasy films. Many people reinvent themselves after undergoing periods of hardship, finding inspiration in the desolation of their experience. These people find opportunities where there seem to be none. Often a person does not know their strengths or abilities until there is an imperative need to overcome a situation. The creative process in itself is alchemy. It is not the picturesque image of a sage in old rags mixing ingredients in a cauldron in days of yore, but the use of one's energy in the practical application of someone's unlimited resources to generate a new life. The raw materials and the secret ingredients are the invisible and intangible resourcefulness of a person of which they might have never been aware of until the moment in which it becomes a necessity. It is action, being proactive; being open to what it might bring. Creative energy is a powerful source of self-support. The use and practice of it increases confidence and improves self-esteem. It is the vital energy to create a new reality, a new you. Feelings do change as we connect to it. One feels more adventurous, playful. The predisposition to take risks is higher; entering the unknown becomes familiar, discovering fresh spaces in which a person can reinvent themselves again and again until they find the satisfactory state of being that provides for everything they need.

The image of the artist portrayed as the tortured soul that never finds happiness or stability, may create the illusion of dismantling the theory that this energy could offer an infinite array of possibilities in which one can find their true self. Having an innate ability to connect to an energy or producing artwork should not be confused with happiness. One finds happiness in the process. Artists do tend to navigate darker spaces in which to find different sources of inspiration, concepts and ideas that can be applied to their work. There is also a great deal of self-mythology, as well as the stereotypical belief that an artist must suffer in order to produce a great work of art. Misery is not an essential ingredient to find inspiration, nor to produce work. This is simply another myth. It might create a public persona, but it is not a necessary prerequisite to be an artist. The truth is that no one knows what goes within, but the person who is going through the experience. Tendencies are changing, therefore artists are taking care of themselves. The secret to love and happiness is in the choices we make. What an artist might do is to break their hearts again and again seeking inspiration in the depths of darkness. Heartbreak is not a space that just happens to someone, it is also self-induced. The artist understand that heartbreak is necessary.

Classical music encompasses all the elements of the human experience, as well as all the movements of heart and soul. Beethoven exemplifies the heartbreak, the discontentment of the child, the melancholy for a childhood lost, but also the rebellion that finds its way to a moment of glory and joy. It is the relentless knock on the heart by pain and suffering to find out if someone is home, alive, inspired by the relationship with his father. Bach brings that fullness of the spirit, the movement and the stillness, the reverence and a direct channel to God. God in this case understood as universal energy; the creative source itself. Brahms represents wholeness, everything there is. It is a sense of completeness; the understanding of the soul. The richness in his compositions might be intimidating before the presence of what is whole. A dimension without limitation, a space in which everything is possible. Chopin is the stillness, the movement, the melancholy of the soul. There is the sadness of a solitary soul, but also the anger, the power to rise of the human spirit. Chopin depicts the stages of heartbreak, the melancholy, the sadness, the longing, the loneliness, the pause, the understanding and acceptance. There is pain throughout, but also the energy and joy that leads to the creation of the perfect love poem's final verse. Mozart composes with the energy of the child that continues to thrive and play in each heartbeat, in each note, but also composes with the melancholy, the longing for paradise lost. The unseen, unheard child. All of them, seek love and beauty through longing, the reminiscence of something lost, but which at the same time is still there. Through art each of these composers finds the access to it. In all of them, one can also recognise the intimacy of the relationship with the self, the romance, the pause, the hope, the heartbreak. In all these cases, the heart is the composer.

One can look at the great artists and art and be intimidated by the achievements of others, or to find the synergy, the connection, the complicity; the inspiration. It is a matter of perspective. Art is there to awaken others to a more fulfilling, inspired realities. The choice of classical music in this book is deliberate, as it is conducive, exemplifying the movements of the soul in the human experience, the connection with the creative source. Classical music is a wonderful space for personal transformation that allows the embodiment of limitless possibilities in the human being. In classical music, one finds the balance of movement and stillness, as well as every feeling and emotion. Seeking inspiration in other artists, one can experience the flow of creativity through feeling and emotion. Everyone is a mirror. The purpose of the artist is to inspire the spark in the hearts of people, reason for which artists do tend to dip into darkness, so as to see the light. The longing is already there, in each of us. Finding the heart and courage to seek it is what determines in which state of being one decides to live in.

The creative process might not translate into figurative art, and it does not have to. The aim is to find what is already within, so as to bring a new creation that can be offered to yourself first, then to the world.

In the flow of the creative process, the feeling and its physical manifestation, the creator perceives that the origin of the energy is not the person in itself, but that they are merely the body that channels it. Its nature is universal, an energy to which anyone has access. It belongs to everyone and no one at the same time. It is a humbling experience to perceive that one is not that special after all, and that at the same time, they can bring to the world such beautiful creations.

John Updike claimed that when he sat down to write, someone else took over, and as he finished working, he found writings that surprise him time and again. I go through the same process. I sit down to write losing track of time to find a piece of work by the end of the process. In this state, words and ideas are presented at such speed that it is hard at times to keep up the pace. It is a trance, a moment of co-creation. This reason alone should suffice to convince anyone to keep the receptacle, one's own body, heart and mind in good shape by moving towards healthier choices that contribute to build better personal and collective worlds within this one. Every manifestation of creativity is an offering of one's personal beauty and their gifts to the world. There is an energy that connects everyone. If there is not a sense of unity is due to the fact that society supressed creativity in favour of repetitive and mindless production. Art and the creative process is an act of love to the self, the world and others.

Avoid the usual distractions such a social media. Social media gives the appearance of interaction, but also provokes unwanted thinking due to disagreements with different views. It turns into a constant inner chatter that leads nowhere. Keep yourself disconnected in order to be connected. Social media gives the impression that one is connected, has a social life while interacting with others. This is of course an activity that can be pursued, but one has to recognise that it is also one that takes a lot of energy that usually does not produce anything. It requires constant attention and input of energy from your part. Social media is an example. TV has a similar effect. It does not require interaction, but attention, causing vital energy to drop to low levels, as it is a passive activity. It is better to do nothing than to resort to the illusion of participation. Doing nothing often creates spaces to nurture the self and regain energy. If after a day of interaction through social media there has been no production or a sense of accomplishment, one might what to ask themselves a few questions about the purpose of it. There might not be connection despite the connection. Again, one can recognise this by the feeling that is created. It does create an addiction, requiring others to be responsive at all times.

The constant need to use social media could be a symptom of loneliness, but also a disconnection with the closest environment. An uncomfortable emotion that requires feeling, shadow work. Resisting the temptation to use a distraction to make time pass faster can only bring good results. It helps to familiarise with the self, creating a stronger connection with inner wisdom. In time one gets used to it, loneliness vanishes leaving room for more energising emotions. Needless to say that one does not have to spend all their time alone during this process. Life continues, but it does not have to be the same.

With the end of a relationship comes a great void. The love, support and affection that was there one day is removed the next. Separation can be a violent and shocking movement. It allows plenty of space and time to be alone, but also one might feel inclined to fill it with meaningless activities that once again create the illusion of social acceptance. There is no need to fill the void. The void is created by the disconnection with one's creative energy. The relationship might have caused them to rely alone on their partners for love and energy.

Loneliness never offered good advice to anyone. As everything in life, loneliness is a paradox that requires solitude. In the process of reconnecting with the self, one has to make new choices, so as to obtain positive results. A new life cannot be created by using old models, which obviously did not help in bringing the wanted outcomes. While separation might be heart breaking, a person who is accustomed to make healthy choices will not face this period in desperation. They know there are other possibilities ahead. These choices are not external, but inner resources that allow people to move through life with a good level of functioning. What one can do, anyone else can do in their own unique way. This is a time to nourish the self, not only in terms of intake of solids and liquids, but everything else in their surroundings. It is a matter of filling the void with yourself. Reading a good book serves this purpose, but so does dancing, a walk in the woods, writing a short story or a letter or sketching. Anyone can do yoga at home or meditation. Social interaction also needs to be selective, as to considering and questioning their nature. Is going out to a bar with friends to have a few drinks in order to forget the best option? Probably not. It might be time to meet new people. One turns to friends and acquaintances as the obvious the first choice, as they do have the time and patience to hold a friend going through a heart breaking experience, but not all company serves our best interests, nor everyone can hold such space. Drinking is often used to tame distressing emotions. Letting go is a large part of life. Often, what we see as friendly and familiar is what stops us from having the life we desire. Deep within, everyone knows it. What makes a difference is to either follow instincts or not.

Letting go of someone becomes easier when a stronger sense of self is acquired, seeing their own energy as a creative tool that can be projected into a better future. If nurtured, this energy attracts and creates everything we want. It does not only change feelings, it changes the thinking process. One can then begin to look at life through a different filter and see that everything is possible. Unfortunately, creative energy has been buried in the hearts of humanity for centuries. The results are insultingly obvious. Everyone can see the world we have created and continue to allow, as well as the negative and damaging results that has on the general population. It is not a creative world we live in. Energy is wasted in copying what already exists, bringing new technology that is hardly used for creative purposes and that is often focused on causing death and destruction. If there is no sense of unity and peace in the world is due to lack of creativity and personal expression. The true human resources which lie deep within each individual are wasted. First, let's begin with the self, then we can consider fixing the world. Often people feel the urge to fix the world, as the belief is that if the world presents the outer expression of what one desires, they will be happy.

The process is embody the desire finding an outlet, and lead with it, which is what eventually helps to fix the world around us, giving it the expression and form one wants. Trying to fix the world is exhausting. It is a process that never ends, as there is always something or someone else to fix. We can only improve ourselves, and through example inspire others to do so themselves.

To assist in the re-emergence of creative energy, choosing what kind of other energies are allowed in someone's life makes a substantial difference. Energies are transformative. When recognised and allowed to flow, the environment improves. Take a closer look at the company you keep, what enters the body and how time is spent and where. Alcohol, junk food, porn or TV watching are to be avoided. A new life and a new state of being require different activities and ways to engage with life. It is not possible to create certain energies while still connected to negative influences. At this point one must look out for the voice and cunny advice of ego. Ego finds all sorts of reasons to validate one more drink, another casual sex encounter without intimacy or connection or an unhealthy diet. Rules apply to everyone, but not to ego. Ego rationalises that knowing the theory and talking about it the job is done. It has no integrity. Being aware of the steps or the knowledge of the process does not make any difference if one is not fully engaged and prepared to take action. A writer can either write a book or talk about writing a book. There is a significant difference. It is no longer about seeking acceptance from others, but to accept one's uniqueness, to find the inner strength and confidence to express it deliberately and unapologetically in creative ways. The information provided in this book can probably be found in different sources. Perhaps in this text it is concise, as the purpose is to point out steps that help the process. But is also experience and personal knowledge. Knowledge is powerful when shared. However, the point that is being made here is that many people are aware of much if not all of this information, but for varied reasons do not take a proactive approach in their transformation. Whether one is not uncomfortable enough in the comfort zone or afraid to enter the unknown, we can only create a fulfilling reality by moving in the right direction. The use of the imagination, as well as to rescue long forgotten dreams is a personal decision that everyone either makes or not. When someone decides to fully embrace life and embody their true potential is a personal choice. If the spark is not here yet, it can be found in the creative process. The process is to ignite and feed the magnetic energy that lies within everyone in order to attract the desired reality.

Letting go is necessary step in order to reunite with the twin flame. It is a decision made with the heart and with the entire body through feeling and emotion, not one that can be made with the mind. Everything that the mind decides in this process is a product of ego. Create and let go of what might come out of it. One cannot let go of a lover or the idea of a twin flame while feeling heartbroken, although steps can be made by setting an intention. It is impossible to love with a broken heart. This is only an illusion. Letting go becomes a key element when the death of the physical person occurs. In the event of death there is despair, a void that can never be filled again or a longing that will never be fulfilled. However delicate this subject is, not everything is lost. Twin flames have a unique way to carry themselves. They are magic. Their presence alone is vibrant, magnetic. This is something that others can see, but that only you can feel. In all relationships too much importance is given to the other person in the process of co-creation, as if you alone were not capable of such magic. It is true that in relationships the act of co-creating is more dynamic, fulfilling and entertaining. It is fuelled by love and happiness, two energies that only a fewer number have managed to accomplish by themselves. It is also true that as human beings we are meant to love and co-create, to share life with others. Society promotes the selfish idea of the individual or self-idolisation instead. Love and relationships provide for these wonderful platforms in which everything is possible. When facing the death of the physical person, there is the unavoidable mourning period, in which someone may take as long as they wish in order to reconcile with the loss. There is no time limit. This fact should not be a deterrent for anyone to stop living. Mourning someone's death, as everything else has a natural course. Anyone would know when they are ready to leave this space. When someone lives with the belief that the deceased is in fact their twin flame, it might be difficult to reconcile with the idea that there is love after love or that it is not possible to find a deep, magical connection with another. This is due to the belief that the twin flame is love's final destination, a subject that has been discussed in 'Debunking the Myth.' In this case, letting go is a matter or removing this belief, as it is indeed possible to love someone else, as it is to create a wonderful reality with them. Nothing belongs to us, nothing can be controlled. Looking at others while still holding this belief will never allow anyone to appear fully, and one will never see who they truly are. Comparison ends killing all passion. One needs to make sure that they are ready to open their heart to love and to the other person. There is no need to remove the memory of the twin flame, but one has to accept the end of the relationship, understanding that it is the beginning of a relationship with the self, and perhaps with someone else in time or maybe even with the same person.

Giving too much credit to a twin flame or to the presence of a lover to bring to life the magnetism and energy of a relationship leads people to undervalue their own abilities. It is a confusing and misleading belief. None of the magic and synergy in the relationship would have appeared without you. The feeling and emotion created in each memory with a lover holds an energy that only two people have experienced. Choose your memory, choose your energy. The energy is always there, as so it is the memory. Romantic relationships offer the opportunity to reconnect with these energies through love, feelings and emotions, but love is the energy that you want to focus on at this moment. As a reminder, falling in love is the reconnection with the emotion and the state of being, an energy that is always within each person. A lover in this case facilitates the feeling, but one has to take ownership of love. It belongs to you. Every energy, feeling and emotion that appear due to the multiple experiences that a couple go through is already within a person. Relationships allow to drop barriers and remove inhibitions in order to go through these experiences. As death occurs, by revisiting memories one can also revisit their energies, feelings and emotions, so as to integrate each one into their being. It is taking conscious ownership of something that was already here, not there; something that belongs to you, not to another. The relationship was a gift, and so was their love. The process of integration is similar to the creative process, only that more powerful, deeper and invigorating, especially when the recent experience is the death of a lover. Memories remain sacred spaces that no one would tarnish with external, damaging energies. Love and the sacredness of such memories only allow loving energies to flow. These are energies that anyone can access again through memory and feeling, bring them back to life and absorb the energy in the process. The familiarity to each energy is a reminder that they were with you all along, and that now you recognise it as your own. This process allows to feel the other person even when they are no longer present. In time, one acknowledges the moment in which to let go.

Choosing yourself, your wellbeing and the will to manifest a fulfilling life are essential parts in the process of letting go. This concept has been repeated throughout this book due to its importance and the inner guidance that comes as a result of such decision. The purpose is to feel better, to gain an inner strength that finally allows the courage to recognise that you are enough as you are. It is a way to become a leader; in your life and choices. The choices you would not make for your loved ones, should not be made for yourself. Wise decisions make you your best friend, a better lover, a best parent to yourself, a better person. This is a reality without self-deprecating thoughts, a sense of wholeness and a strong belief and determination in one's own possibilities. We can be thankful to an ex-lover for having touched our lives, hearts and souls, to then let them go knowing that the best is yet to come, and that we as individuals are the creators of our own reality. This is only possible through feeling. When it appears, it is easy to recognise. The creative process is the celebration of the self, the rebellion against those forces and voices that repeatedly tell us that we are not enough, by embodying the truth that is hidden within; the opposite of what you might have been told throughout life. The voice within that repeats that you are not enough, it is not your true voice.

The true twin flame, what you really are looking for, is you, and you alone. It has always been you. The physical twin flame, as in a person is real. They may appear or they may not. As described in previous chapters their role in someone's lives is to help and support the journey of self-discovery. Meeting them accelerates the process for one simple reason. Twin flames do not cause harm to the other deliberately. Hurt may come as a results of the intensity, feelings and emotions, or due to an emotional reaction to a situation or a strong sense of self-preservation. The reason one is so attracted to the other, as well as the strong, deep connection is due to the fact that their energy matches the energy that you already have within, but from which you have been disconnected, not being aware that it was with you all along. The twin flame is the balancing of energies; the male and female energy. The balancing of these energies allows you to feel the twin flame at any time regardless of their location, as it allows to project energy to any part of the world as a communication system. Each flame is an energy. Both lie within you. The reunion is the feeling and embodiment of such energies at once in the present moment. By letting go and engaging in the creative process of rediscovering the self, these energies are balanced, bringing a sensation of wholeness and fulfilment that no one else could produce. In a world that lacks creativity, and in which most people believe creativity is not an innate trait in them, energy can only be balanced by supporting and expanding what is missing. Art or creativity does not have to be commercial a commercial purpose. If a commercial outlet is possible, it is a plus, but looking at every aspect of life from a monetary value interferes with the process. This is one of the erroneous beliefs imposed by society and patriarchy, that only that which is created for the purpose of a financial transaction has value. You are the most valuable masterpiece you will ever own.

It does not necessarily mean that the separation with the twin flame will occur regardless on one's efforts. Creating a healthy and successful relationship is also possible with the physical twin flame, even when there is a temporary separation. Everything is possible.

Changing beliefs is part of the process of life, so as not to remain stagnant, allowing energetic space for personal growth. People who become old in their 20's or 40's do so due to energetic stagnation and a set of beliefs that do not allow expansion. Reaching the sense of wholeness and mastering creative energies open opportunities to create deep and loving connections with other people. Life does not end after the twin flame. It begins. One of the reasons why the physical twin flame might leave the relationship is because they might have made a strong commitment to their self-development. This commitment is energetic. Energy decisions and intentions are different from those made with the mind, following an energetic connection to different places or other people. It is the nature of adventure. These intentions are often made during childhood when the connection with the true self is stronger. Many may have forgotten. Others follow their heart. You may know people who wander from place to place, from relationship to relationship never settling for anything or anyone, but that somehow always land on their feet. They are answering the call of the heart and soul. Sometimes a self-destructive life is a creative one as what is created is a permanent sense of freedom, a deep, powerful connection with the inner self. Their lives might not make sense to others as their product of the creation is neither tangible, nor material. Freedom never takes that form. They may seem lost to others, they are not. They just live and enjoy the sense of wonder in the adventure, and the uncertainty of not knowing.

As per changing beliefs, it might be time to challenge that one that tells you that you are not enough, as well as the negative voice within that always finds reasons to keep repeating the same verbatim. If you have been loved or are loved at the moment, it is because you are enough.

"Be careful what you wish for", is not just a myth, but a desire that might come true. How one wishes and with what energy is crucial to the outcome. Energy calls and attracts desires: people, places and experiences. What we must know and remember is that during the process of self-discovery a powerful learning curb takes place. Life in itself is a process of transformation. We either live it or wither while we continue existing. This knowledge has to be made conscious as it is a powerful tool to create a wonderful reality, to attract the love we want, as well as a joyful life. Creative energy is a magnet. As it is a feeling, it does produce incredible insights and inspiration. It transforms life, as one no longer has time for habits nor types of behaviour that do not serve the completeness of the human spirit. It is a natural device that either excludes or includes by feeling and intuition. This energy is an endless source of wisdom. When reawakened, an individual would seek new challenges by creating opportunities, including a more realistic lover with whom to share the process. Love is not reduced to one person only. This is a fabricated myth that if not removed from the mind takes over the entire being, creating dissociation from the body and the true nature of the self. In addition, it creates an unfulfilling life, disappointment and perhaps a permanent state of depression.

There are many people with whom one could create magnetic connections, even more exciting and encouraging than the created with the twin flame, although first, one must to reconnect with a sense of wholeness. The feeling that we are enough takes over. Then everything is possible.

In my practice I work with numerous clients. The initial consultations mostly cover situations in which people are standing on a fence: unfulfilling relationships or the possibility to begin a new one. Although it varies according to the person, it is common to observe low self-esteem, lack of confidence, depression, guilt or shame as the majority of cases involve to give bad news to someone else, excluding them from their lives. Everything changes when clients choose themselves deciding to reconnect with the true essence. From then on, the process of rejuvenation through a creative process and self-love brings them to the beautiful reality of themselves.

In the past I worked with a client tormented by doubts in relationships. After a few weeks of indecision and without any mentioning of the proces or creating her own reality, as she was not ready, she took the decision herself. The next session she was in a state of bliss and to this day. Romantic relationships passed to a secondary place in her life, something that she might welcome, but that is not a necessity and in opposition to what she had been led to believe all her life. One of the most powerful statements I heard from a client, and I heard many, was her response when questioned about love. "I will know", she said. What this feeling brings is this; a sense of knowing. It goes deep, and resonates powerfully throughout the entire being.

Perhaps the last point to cover is that when feeling stuck in this process consulting a professional helps in gaining clarity and guidance. Unfortunately, it is common in people to wait until the relationship has deteriorated beyond the point of repair, or has even ended before people action is taken. At this point it is still possible to deal with the issues and deeper traumas that are likely to be the cause of these situations, but too late for reconciliation. This book carries a strong intention to bring awareness of all the issues that might be presented in relationships, as well as all the motions that couple might go through if one wants to be the leader in their experience without any assistance. I am a great believer in the do-it-yourself-approach, as I believe that everyone is a leader. From personal experience I know that sometimes all it takes is to point out their innate leadership skills to someone. Everyone was born with all the tools necessary to create the most outstanding version of themselves. How long one wants to continue listening to the noise of the world while not practising the wonders of the self is a question that only you can answer. Choose yourself and you will get to where you want to be. Everything you seek is already here, and it is possible.

Every step taken in the direction of self-discovery is a step closer to love with another, twin flame or not. This concept might be difficult to understand, but by choosing yourself in each step you are also giving a step closer to what you want to manifest in your life. It magnetises what you want. Every amount of energy dedicated to self-development with discipline and commitment takes you there. It is possible that it is not manifested as imagined, but it appears eventually. If one thing one could indulge more in, that is in their own desires, in developing the ability to ask and receive. Whether this is to bring back a long lost lover, starting a business, reshape your body or to write that book everyone has within, the answer is in you. It is a process in which one finds answers without questions by living deliberately and with passion. Just ask with your heart.

There is not a standard formula to do this kind of work. The purpose of the creative process is that everyone learns to develop a set of skills that serves their needs. What might work for some or how it works, might not do so for others. Flexibility extends as far as one allows it. It is limitless. The different elements and steps are described in this book. How far or deep anyone wants to go, or when to use it, is a personal choice that no one can make but you. The journey into the unknown becomes familiar as one advances in the process. What might be reason for fear today, may turn into a reason to thrive tomorrow. There is nothing to fix. You are not broken. Focus on creating yourself and everything else will be fixed naturally. When energy is focused on yourself instead of on others, it creates presence. Presence is you expanding. Presence is you, it is love, magnetising anything you want. It is a magnet that speaks from the heart. It is a language that you speak and that the world wants to hear.

Printed in Great Britain
by Amazon